A Dynamic Use of Survey Data and High Frequency Model Forecasting

A Dynamic Use of Survey Data and High Frequency Model Forecasting

Yoshihisa Inada

Konan University, Japan & Asia Pacific Institute of Research, Japan

World Scientific

NEW JERSEY • LONDON • SINGAPORE • BEIJING • SHANGHAI • HONG KONG • TAIPEI • CHENNAI • TOKYO

Published by

World Scientific Publishing Co. Pte. Ltd.
5 Toh Tuck Link, Singapore 596224
USA office: 27 Warren Street, Suite 401-402, Hackensack, NJ 07601
UK office: 57 Shelton Street, Covent Garden, London WC2H 9HE

Library of Congress Cataloging-in-Publication Data
Names: Inada, Yoshihisa, 1952– editor.
Title: A dynamic use of survey data and high frequency model forecasting / edited by
Yoshihisa Inada (Konan University, Japan & Asia Pacific Institute of Research, Japan).
Description: New Jersey : World Scientific, [2018]
Identifiers: LCCN 2017051223 | ISBN 9789813232365 (hc : alk. paper)
Subjects: LCSH: Economic forecasting--Mathematical models. | Econometrics.
Classification: LCC HB3730 .D96 2018 | DDC 330.01/5195--dc23
LC record available at https://lccn.loc.gov/2017051223

British Library Cataloguing-in-Publication Data
A catalogue record for this book is available from the British Library.

For any available supplementary material, please visit
http://www.worldscientific.com/worldscibooks/10.1142/10772#t=suppl

Desk Editors: Suraj Kumar/Philly Lim

Typeset by Stallion Press
Email: enquiries@stallionpress.com

About the Author

Professor **Yoshihisa Inada** received his B.A., M.A. and Ph.D. in Economics from Kobe University in 1976, 1978 and 1992, respectively. He is currently the Director at the Center for Quantitative Economic Analysis (CQEA), Asia Pacific Institute of Research, and is also the Vice-President of Konan University since 2014. He served as a lecturer at Kobe-Gakuin University in 1981 and then became an Assistant Professor in 1984. He has also held Visiting Researcher status at the Research Institute of the Economic Planning Agency, Institute of Developing Economies, The University of Pennsylvania and The International Center for the Study of East Asian Development. He was an Associate Professor at Ritsumeikan University, and subsequently was appointed as a full Professor at Konan University in 1995, where he still serves today. He was elected Dean of Konan University, a post which he served from 2007 to 2009, and subsequently was appointed Councillor to the President. He was the Director of the Frontier Research Organization for New Themes at Konan University from 2010 to 2012. He was a Research Director at Kansai Institute for Social and Economic Research (2011) and a Director of Research at Asia Pacific Institute of Research (2011–2014). Professor Inada has numerous publications to his credit, including a chapter in the book *Environmental Governance for Sustainable Development: East Asian Perspectives*, published by United Nations University Press, a chapter in the book *The Making of National Economic Forecasts*, published by Edward Elgar and another chapter in the book *Macroeconometric Modeling of Japan*, published by World Scientific Publishing Company. Professor Inada mainly concentrates on the areas of Macroeconomics, Applied Econometrics and Economic Forecasting and teaches students in these areas.

List of Contributors

Ryoh Ogawa

Associate Professor, Graduate School of Economics, Osaka City University, 3-3-138 Sugimoto, Sumiyoshi-ku, Osaka, 558-8585, Japan

Hajime Watabe

Senior Manager, BtoB Unit, Digital Business, Nikkei Inc. & Principal Economist, Japan Center for Economic Research, Japan

Nariyasu Yamasawa

Professor, Faculty of Management, Atomi University
1-9-6 Nakano, Niiza-shi, Saitama 352-8501, Japan

Yuzo Kumasaka

President and CEO, IT Economy Advisors, LLC, USA

Introduction: Background to a High-Frequency Model Forecast

Yoshihisa Inada

Konan University and the Asia Pacific Institute of Research

This publication, which is made up of five chapters, investigates the accuracy and dynamic performance of a high-frequency forecast model for the Japanese and United States economies based on the Current Quarter Model (CQM) or high frequency model (HFM) developed by the late Professor Emeritus Lawrence R. Klein. It also presents a survey of recent developments in high-frequency forecasts and gives an example of application of the CQM model in forecasting gross regional products (GRPs).

Two of the authors, Yuzo Kumazaka and Yoshihisa Inada, studied under Professor Klein from early 1980s, participating in the Professor's research and learning much from him about the field of forecasting. Professor Klein was the first person in the world to develop a macroeconometric model for the US economy. He used this model (the Klein–Goldberger model) to effectively respond to the debate regarding whether the US economy would experience a second Great Depression after the Second World War. Subsequently, in his position at Pennsylvania University, he conducted joint research projects with researchers from across the world and used trade matrices to combine macroeconometric models for individual countries and develop a model for the global economy. Further, as the Chair of the "Consortium Project LINK", he made numerous policy recommendations at the United Nations. He also started a private forecasting company and developed many econometric models for businesses, including the WEFA model. The recent publication *Klein's Last Quarterly Econometric Model of the United States* (World Scientific) presents an overview of the WEFA model and its historical significance.

While tutoring many disciples, Professor Klein stood at the forefront of the forecasting world as the pioneer and leading proponent of the macroeconometric model. As such, his forecasting techniques and views were subject to various critiques, such as the Lucas critique (1976). Robert Lucas argued that exogenous variables estimated using vector autoregression (VAR) and a suitable reduced form model is sufficient for econometric forecasting. However, Klein stressed the importance of the structural model and continued to focus on improving forecast accuracy. For example, he noted that the arbitrariness of adjusting constants to improve the initial accuracy of the forecast was problematic. As a response to the Lucas critique, he suggested a practical method for solving this problem. He put that idea, the CQM, into practice for the first time in 1990. Klein even had grand plans to develop a CQM for the world economy in the manner of the econometric model he developed for Project LINK. The CQM is a forerunner for the nowcasting models used today, such as "GDPNow" and "GDP Tracker".

The authors' experience using Professor Klein's CQM forecasting technique over a period of more than 25 years has created a large volume of spillover. The impetus for this publication is the desire to detail some of these experiences and the achievements of the model.

1. Methodology of High-Frequency Model Forecasting

Klein edited a book detailing various countries' high-frequency forecasting models, *The Making of National Economic Forecasts*, in 2009. Chapter 1, Klein set two guiding hypotheses about national economies in its background:

1. The national economy is viewed as a highly multivariate macroeconomic concept.

2. The ultimate test of the validity of economic propositions is the accuracy of forecasts.

The second hypothesis here is particularly important. Klein argued that the effects of economic propositions can be forecast, and the ultimate test of the validity of these propositions is the accuracy of these forecasts. Whether or not certain multivariate economic relationships form repeatedly can be forecast by extrapolating from data using a model. There will inherently be a certain degree of forecast error, but current data will verify the model's forecasting potential. The economist must be aware, however, that highly correlated data are not well suited to forecasts because a model's parameters are estimated from past data and estimated so as to make theoretical levels as close to current data levels as possible. These are problems that economists must consider carefully when using high-frequency forecast models. Database systems and repetition of forecasts should be used as strict tests to improve forecast accuracy when extrapolating from past data.

How should the economist, then, go about performing a high-frequency model forecast so as to ensure its high-forecasting potential? Klein summarizes the general procedure for making a high-frequency model forecast of the US economy in the following seven steps (see Klein, 2009, pp. 9–10):

1. Build a database of quarterly and annual macroeconomic data covering the whole economy and some particular trading partners.
2. Build a database of monthly, or more frequent, indicators that are tied to a system performance or of economic interest in their own right.
3. Estimate bridge relations between strategic indicators at high-frequency and elements of national income and product accounts (NIPA), also extended to lower frequency.
4. Each week, some indicators are published in reports, and bridge equations are reestimated and extrapolated over the forecast horizon.
5. Standard NIPA tables are updated and examined for effects on movement of economy.
6. Fresh NIPA tables are analyzed throughout the period of extrapolation. For the USA, the tables provide data for three estimates of gross domestic product (GDP) and two of GDP deflator. One is

demand-side estimate, another is income-side (supply-side) estimate, and third estimate is one obtained by using the principal components of major indicators of GDP and its deflator. The final estimate of GDP and its price deflator forms a simple averages.

7. Interpret results, judge their consistency and plausibility, keeping in mind that the week-to-week changes should nearly always be in historical range.

2. Forecasting Using the Bridge Equation

The method for performing high-frequency model forecasts is determined by the usability of data and the frequency of its release and thus varies from country to country, but fundamentally, high-frequency forecasts are carried out according to the rules set by Klein. As explained in Step 3 above, the bridge equation plays an important role in high-frequency forecasts. National economic statistics, such as quarterly GDP and its components, are estimated from monthly data based on set rules. Bridge equations are used to convert basic monthly data into quarterly data on the national economy. Klein's bridge forecasting method is now being used in nowcasting models such as GDPNow and GDP Tracker.[1]

In the bridge equation forecasts in Step 4, time series analysis methods are used to forecast basic monthly variables 6 months (two quarters) into the future. Time series model forecasts perform to a very high degree of accuracy when the forecast time horizon is set to two quarters.

3. Forecasting Using Principal Components Analysis

As shown in Step 6, along with bridge equations, the principle component analysis model (production-side) also plays an important role in Klein's CQM. The CQM forecasts GDP from three sides. It forecasts the demand

[1] In the abstract of a Working Paper, Higgins explained "This paper documents GDP Now, a 'now casting' model for gross domestic product (GDP) growth that synthesizes the 'bridge equation' approach relating GDP subcomponents to monthly source data with the factor model approach used by Giannone, Reichlin, and Small (2008)". In Patric Higgins (2014), "GDP Now: A Model for GDP 'Now casting'", *FRB of Atlanta Working Paper Series 2014–7*, July 2014.

and income sides of US GDP using bridge equations. The problem, however, is forecasting the production side. By rule, demand and income GDP data are released quarterly, and certain component data are released monthly and available for use. The bridge equations use basic monthly data related to quarterly gross domestic expenditure (GDE) to estimate quarterly GDP. The problem is that data related to production-side GDP are only released once a year. To overcome this problem, Klein hypothesized, according to the principle of equivalence of the three sides of GDP, that GDP is equal to GDE (the data of which is released quarterly), and proposed that GDP be forecast using monthly production-side data. However, unlike in the demand- and income-side bridge equations, there is no concrete correspondence between the monthly production-side data and quarterly GDP component data. Therefore, as shown in Step 6, the third method used is to estimate the GDP and its deflator using indicators with high explanatory power gained from the principle component analysis.

Principal component analysis is a method that is well known in the fields of sociology and psychology. Within the field of econometrics, it is used as a technique for choosing variables so as to prevent multicollinearity (see Maddala (1992)). A brief overview of the method is presented below.

Suppose that there are a certain number (k) of the explanatory variables (x), expressed in the following linear function:

$$z_1 = a_{1,1}x_1 + a_{1,2}x_2 + \cdots\cdots + a_{1,k}x_k$$
$$z_2 = a_{2,1}x_1 + a_{2,2}x_2 + \cdots\cdots + a_{2,k}x_k.$$

Under the condition that $a_{1,1}^2 + a_{1,2}^2 + \cdots + a_{1,k}^2 = 1$, a value for a that gives the maximum variance in z_1 is chosen. z_1, referred to as the first principal component, is a function of x with maximum variance. Next, z_2 is taken to be a linear equation with maximum variance that has no correlation with z_1. It carries the condition that $a_{2,1}^2 + a_{2,2}^2 + \cdots + a_{2,k}^2 = 1$, and is referred to as the second principal component. When this procedure is repeated and the variance of variables z_1, z_2, …, z_k combined, the following equation is satisfied:

$$\mathrm{var}(z_1) + \mathrm{var}(z_2) + \cdots\cdot + \mathrm{var}(z_k) = \mathrm{var}(x_1) + \mathrm{var}(x_2) + \cdots\cdot + \mathrm{var}(x_k).$$

While $x_1, x_2, \ldots, x_k$ are highly correlated, the variables in $z_1, z_2, \ldots, z_k$ have a mutually orthogonal relationship and have no correlation. Instead of regressing y on $x_1, x_2, \ldots, x_k$, we can regress y on $z_1, z_2, \ldots, z_k$ and obtain the same result as before. This is the appealing feature of principal component analysis: it allows for the partial grouping and regression of mutually uncorrelated principal components.

Time series analysis techniques are used to forecast monthly economic variables 6 months into the future in principal component analysis forecasts.

As a final procedure in Step 6, Klein recommends calculating a simple average of the demand-, income- and production-side forecasts as a final estimate of true GDP. He recommends this because the estimates for all the three sides of GDP, each calculated using a different method, have a certain level of statistical discrepancy.

The high-frequency forecast model thus collates estimates of components into an overall estimate for the real GDP for the present quarter on a weekly basis. In other words, the real monthly data released in that week and estimates of monthly data account for changes in forecast levels for GDP and its components for that quarter. This means that the high-frequency forecast model is, unlike other forecast models, extremely dynamic. It provides valuable information that can be used to judge changes in business conditions. Finally, Step 7 stresses that, as stated above, database systems and repetition of forecasts should be used as strict tests to improve forecast accuracy in this method of extrapolation from past data.

4. Forecast Accuracy Does Matter

Kumasaka and Inada, inspired by Professor Klein, both developed high-frequency forecast models based on Klein's techniques. Kumasaka developed a CQM model for the US, while Inada developed a CQM model for Japan. For a period of over a quarter century (from the early 1990s to the present day), they have produced forecasts every week and tested the accuracy of these on a quarterly basis, focusing on using data systems and repeated forecasts to improve accuracy.

The appealing features of the CQM, verified by comparing the Japanese CQM with market consensus, are as follows:

1. The CQM forecast is dynamic and its accuracy rises further as the basic monthly data of current quarter GDP become available. It has been understood that the CQM forecast can lead the market consensus for 2–3 months and offer an accurate forecast.
2. Moreover, the consensus forecast has been influenced by the mood of the market though it is stable, as some examples show.
3. The CQM forecast model, which deals with economic statistics objectively and judges by the way of "Go by the Numbers", is an effective method for economists and decision makers.

As a final note in this brief overview, it should be noted that the CQM has generated significant spillover in its quarter-century history. Part of this influence will be introduced in this volume. In addition to its application in national economic forecasts, the CQM has also been useful in the development of regional econometric models. The following chapters contain three survey-based essays and studies of the application of the CQM idea.

References

Giannone, D., L. Reichlin and Small D. (2008) "Nowcasting: The Real-Time Informational Content of Macroeconomic Data," *Journal of Monetary Economics*, No. 55, pp. 665–676.

Higgins, P. C. (2014) GDP Now: A Model for GDP "Now casting," *FRB of Atlanta Working Paper Series 2014–7*, July.

Inada, Y. (2010) "High Frequency Model vs. Consensus Forecast," in L. R. Klein (ed.) *The Econometric Modeling of Japan*, World Scientific Publisher.

Klein, L. R. and J. Y. Park (1995) "The University of Pennsylvania Model for High-Frequency Economic Forecasting," *Economic and Financial Modeling*, Autumn, pp. 95–146.

Klein, L. R. (2009) "Background to National Economic Forecasts and the High-frequency Model of the USA," in L. R. Klein (ed.) *The Making of National Economic Forecasts*, Edward Elgar, pp. 1–26.

Klein, L. R. (2018) Klein's Lats Quarterly Econometric Model of the United States Wharton Quarterly Econometric Model-Mark 10, edited by S. Ichimura, S. Kinoshita & M. Yamada, World Scientific.

Lucas, R. E. (1976) "Econometric Policy Evaluation: A Critique," in K. Brunner and A. Meltzer (eds.) *The Phillips Curve and Labor Markets*, Carnegie-Rochester Conference Series on Public Policy, Vol 1. Amsterdam North Holland.

Maddala, G. S. (1992) *Introduction to Econometrics*, 2nd ed. Macmillan.

Contents

Chapter 1

A Survey of Flash Data and Nowcasting in Japan

Nariyasu Yamasawa

Atomi University

1. Introduction

This study surveys two statistical approaches to making flash assessments of the real economy. The first approach involves making flash estimations using official statistics. The second approach involves making high-frequency forecasts using various econometric techniques.

A major problem with economic statistics is that the process of releasing them is slow, generally taking at least 1 month to gather, compile, and verify data. Compiling secondary statistics, such as gross domestic product (GDP) statistics, takes yet more time.

Delays in monitoring economic situations can negatively affect policymakers. In 2014, Japan's Prime Minister Shinzo Abe stated that the government would decide whether to raise consumption tax based on the performance of GDP in the July–September quarter. However, GDP data became available only on November 17, 2014, which meant that the government was able to first assess the economic situation 2 months after the relevant period.

Of course, the Statistics Bureau makes efforts to release data promptly, and data today are released faster than in the 1990s. However, there are limits to these flash releases, and to grasp the actual state of the economy sooner, it is necessary to forecast. A variety of research studies have been published about high-frequency forecasts using monthly and daily variables. Researchers have attempted to make monthly GDP forecasts using many different methods, including the current quarter model (CQM), the monthly data model, and the factor model. In addition, inflation forecasts, which are important from the viewpoint of monetary policy, are conducted by many institutions. In this chapter, we will examine these forecast techniques and how they are being used today.

2. Releasing Flash Data

2.1. Delays in obtaining economic data

Weather forecasts and economic forecasts are similar. However, one significant difference between the two is that it takes a long time to obtain economic data, whereas we can obtain weather data immediately. It is possible to gather data on temperature, humidity, and wind speed for each city in real time and use these data to make short-term forecasts. The website of Japan's Meteorological Agency shows radar "nowcasting" for rain, thunder, and tornados. This comprises forecasts of rain, thunder, and tornados from 1 hour before to 1 hour after the present time, in 10-minute intervals.

On the other hand, although market-related data can be obtained almost in real time, it takes longer for industrial production and sales data to be released. Some data are released only quarterly and some detailed data are released only yearly.

Economic policy has to be developed as soon as possible after the economic events. However, there are three kinds of lags in relation to executing economic policy: Recognition, execution, and effect lags. First, a "recognition lag" is a delayed recognition of changes in economic conditions. Second, an "execution lag" is a delayed development of economic policy because of the policymaking procedure. Third, an "effect lag" is a delay in the time taken for economic policy to produce actual outcomes.

The delayed release of economic data is one of the reasons why recognition lag occurs. Policymakers have to use past economic data when they develop economic policy and this is referred to, rather sardonically, as "driving a car by looking in the rearview mirror".

2.2. Moving towards flash estimates

Recently, there has been a gradual increase in the release of flash estimates. GDP is a useful statistical measure for business cycle analysis; there is a strong need to release this information quickly, and the Statistics Bureau of Japan (part of the Ministry of Internal Affairs and Communications) has made efforts to do so.

Flash estimates are statistical data that are released quickly in substitution of statistics that are more accurate but released later. For example, the Statistics Bureau originally calculated GDP statistics by using data sources like the "Industry Statistics" of the Ministry of Economy, Trade and Industry (METI) and by studying the inflow and outflow of over 2000 commodities. Moreover, the bureau develops GDP statistics using three approaches: the production-, income-, and expenditure-side approaches. In addition, these statistics are designed to obey the three-sided equivalence principle, so the GDP figure that each approach gives must be the same.

Because the statistics are annual, the Cabinet Office compiles a flash quarterly estimate from only the expenditure side. This estimate is created by substituting quarterly statistics for annual statistics, such as the quarterly Household Survey, the Index of Industrial Production, and Financial Statements Statistics.

The Statistics Bureau made revisions in August 2002 that were central to the improvement of Japan's flash GDP estimates. In that month, the bureau revised the way it made flash estimates by incorporating not only the demand-side but also supply-side statistics into its calculations. In addition, they published these estimates earlier than before. Specifically, before the revision, GDP statistics were released 2 months and 1 week after the relevant period, and after the revision, the first estimates were released 1 month and 2 weeks after, and the second estimates were released 2 months and 10 days after. Although there continues to be a problem in that the revisions that occurs between the first and second estimates is often large, METI's effort to release the statistics earlier is commendable.

Japan is behind the rest of the world in that it does not yet release flash estimates of the supply side and income-side of its GDP. Most OECD countries make flash estimates of their supply-side and income-side GDPs according to the three-sided equivalence principle (Table 1), the three sides being production, distribution, and expenditure. Japan's Cabinet Office has noted that it is behind in releasing production and distribution estimates and is seeking to improve its estimates by including quarterly estimates of these aspects of the GDP after its next revision of the base year (planned for 2016).

2.3. Data revision problems

Flash estimates of GDP provide useful information about business conditions, but they also have problems. Because flash estimates are not made using the original data that are used to make final estimates, data revisions are unavoidable. Moreover, final estimates are not literally final and can be changed. Statistics change when statistics bureaux revise the base year or the deflator, or when they change from using a fixed price method to a chained price method to calculate the real GDP.

Table 1. Comparison of quarterly flash GDP estimates

	Production		Distribution		Expenditure	
	Real	Nominal	Real	Nominal	Real	Nominal
Japan	–	–	–	–	○	○
United Kingdom	○	△	△	○	○	○
Germany	△	○	–	○	△	○
France	○	○	–	○	○	○
United States	○	○	△	○	○	○
Canada	○	–	–	○	○	○
Australia	○	–	○	○	○	○

Note: ○ Available, △ Partly Available, – Not Available

Source: The Cabinet Office (2014), "Research meeting on the next base year revision of National Accounts," 10th meeting, material 2

The data that can be obtained now is called real-time data, and it should be taken into account that policy judgments depend on real-time data. The OECD maintains a public database of real-time data and releases explanations of how it revises those data. For example, the OECD should theoretically only have one real GDP growth rate dataset for Japan in FY 1997, but this dataset was revised several times (Figure 1). The OECD first published Japan's FY1997 GDP growth as –0.8%, but in July 1998, it revised this figure to 0.5% and subsequently to almost 0% in 2014. In 1998, the fact that the GDP growth rate was negative made people believe that business conditions were poor, whereas it turned out that the growth rate was approximately zero. Thus, there is a risk in using real-time data to make judgments.

Researchers have attempted to investigate how data are revised from various viewpoints. A 2007 issue of the "National Account Quarterly" contained a special feature on this so-called "revision study". Kawagoe (2007) studied how Japan's real GDP was revised by dividing the period from the first quarter of 1994 to the third quarter of 2003 into two periods, namely, before and after the fourth quarter of 1998. It was found that the real GDP growth rate in the first period (based on chained 1995 prices) slowed from 1.5% to 0.9%, while the real GDP growth rate in the second period (based on chained 2000 prices) increased from 0.9% to 1.3%.

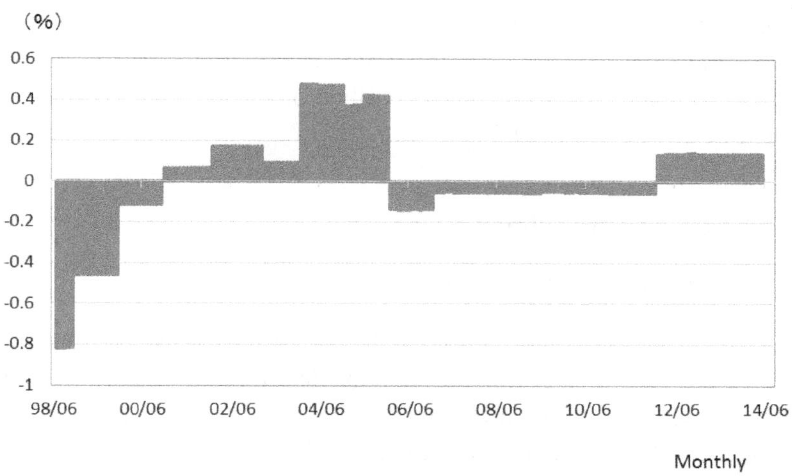

Figure 1. Change of the growth rate of real GDP in FY1997

Source: OECD Original Release Data and Revisions Database

2.4. Noise or news

The nature of the revision from flash estimates to final estimates has been discussed since the 1980s. The need for flash estimates is strong among market investors, but on the other hand, less credible data cause confusion. This problem is discussed as the problem of "noise or news" (Mankiw and Shapiro, 1986). Mankiw and Shapiro describe revisions that include measurement errors as "revisions based on noise". They occur when fewer statistics are used to calculate a flash estimate than the amount used to calculate the final estimate, or when industrial classifications within those statistics are rougher than those of the final estimate. On the other hand, they call flash estimates that are designed as good forecasts of the final estimates "revisions based on news". Further changes to these only occur when news emerges that could not have been known at the time the flash estimate was released. A revision based on news is a flash estimate that is considered to be the best and most desirable forecast of the final estimate possible at the time it was made. A revision based on noise is a flash estimate that is considered to have been produced from unreliable statistics.

Komaki (2005) studied the nature of GDP flash estimates in Japan, and concluded that GDP statistics are revised based on noise. He conducted rational expectation tests of flash estimates, such as bias and efficiency tests, and found that flash estimates of the GDP are different entities to final estimates. Komaki argued that flash estimates are insufficient for indicating the "true GDP" (which Komaki presupposes that final estimates indicate), so people should utilize other statistics, such as stock prices, to find this "true GDP".

3. High-Frequency Model Forecasts

3.1. Complements of actual data

It takes time to gather and compile data for earlier release, in addition to effort on the part of the Statistics Bureau. In cases in which it is impossible to release data more quickly, researchers attempt to forecast the data.

The Statistics Bureau does, in a sense, forecast some part of the "final" statistics it releases, such as GDP statistics. Making "final flash estimates" is a similar process to refining forecast statistics. For example, the main difference between the first and second flash GDP estimates is the way that capital investment is calculated. The Statistics Bureau makes the first flash estimate of capital investment based on METI's "Index of Industrial Shipment of Capital Goods", whereas it makes its second estimate based on the Ministry of Finance's "Financial Statements Statistics of Corporations". In a sense, the Statistics Bureau forecasting capital investment using the Index of Industrial Shipment of Capital Goods before the Financial Statements Statistics of Corporations are published is akin to using a proxy variable to forecast it.

For the first flash estimate, only 2 months of balance of payments data of the relevant quarter have been published. The data of the third month are forecast. For example, for the July–September estimate of GDP, the balance of payments data are available only for July and August, and the Statistics Bureau must forecast figures for September.

3.2. Quick estimation forecast

Quick estimation (QE) is a quarterly flash estimate of real GDP. QE is a very popular forecast and many organizations often make it public. The Japan Center for Economic Research gathers QE forecasts every month and publishes them as "Economy, Society, and Policy (ESP) forecasts".

Takao Komine of Hosei University, formerly chief economist of the Japan Center for Economic Research, coined the term "super short-term forecasts" for QE forecasts. Komine developed this term in the late 1980s in his book, "Introduction to New Business Cycle Observation Methods" (*Nihon Hyoronsha*), in which he classified economic forecasts into short-term, medium-term, and long-term forecasts. He defined short-term forecasts as forecasts of the economy 2 or 3 years ahead, medium-term forecasts as forecasts of the economy about 5 years ahead, and long-term forecasts as forecasts of the economy several decades ahead. His medium-term forecasts focus mainly on industrial structure forecasts and long-term forecasts focus mainly on population forecasts. Furthermore, he defined super short-term forecasts as those for the quarter ahead.

This classification of economic forecasts has been followed by other research institutes. They also consider medium-term forecast as those that focus mainly on industrial structure forecasts, long-term forecasts as those that focus mainly on population forecasts, and short-term forecasts as those that focus on the turning points of business cycles. The only difference in terminology is that most institutions call forecasts of the upcoming quarter as "QE forecasts" instead of "super short-term forecasts".

3.3. Bridge equation: Current quarter model

A popular method of making QE forecasts involves using bridge equations. GDP is quarterly data, but monthly data can be used when compiling some of the statistics needed to forecast GDP. If we change quarterly and monthly data into percentages of annual data, and make that quarterly data the dependent variable Q_t and monthly data the independent variable M_t, we can use the following bridge equation:

$$Q_t = \alpha + \beta \times M_t + e_t, \qquad (1)$$

where α and β are coefficients, e_t is the residual, and M_t is an average of 3 months of data.

The CQM is a forecast method that involves using bridge equations. The method was developed by Lawrence Klein of University of Pennsylvania. If we have M_t for the January–March quarter, then we can estimate Q_t for that quarter. If we have data only for January, Klein suggests forecasting M_t for February and March using time-series analysis. After the release of February data, Klein recommends revising the dataset, forecasting M_t for March, and estimating the first-quarter GDP.

In practice, Klein's forecast method takes into consideration not only the demand side but also the supply side and the income side. In addition, Klein uses many monthly datasets to estimate quarterly GDP data. Regarding the applications of the CQM, Yuzo Kumasaka of IT Economy Advisers LLC has released forecasts of the GDP growth rate of the United States using the CQM, while Yoshihisa Inada of Konan University has made weekly CQM forecasts of Japan's GDP for 20 years (Figure 2).

Inada (2013) argues that CQM forecasts are quicker and more accurate than the market consensus.

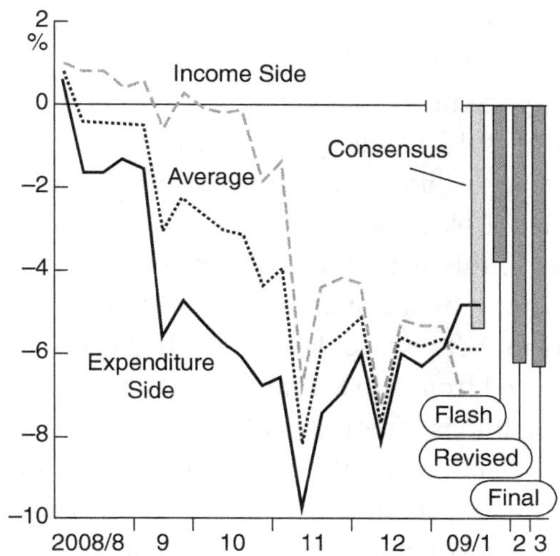

Figure 2. CQM forecasts of United States real economic growth rates in October–December 2008 (seasonally adjusted quarterly growth of per annum rates)

3.4. Accuracy of super short-term forecasts

In this section, we will investigate the accuracy of super short-term, or QE, forecasts. Private forecasting companies have almost the same information, and each organization is aware of how to make super short-term forecasts of GDP to some degree. However, there is disparity between each company's forecast results because these companies do not have perfect information about how to make QE forecasts and they still rely heavily on guesswork. The super short-term forecasts these companies make are seldom accurate, and sometimes, their poor forecasts confuse the financial market.

According to Saito (2012), the margin of error of independent forecasts is very large. Saito found that the absolute average error of the real GDP growth rate was 1.08% from 2000 to 2012. Furthermore, Saito found that the probability of forecasts being within a 0.5% range of the actual GDP was only about 20%.

The announcement of the real GDP growth rate for the third quarter of 2014 was watched with keen interest because Prime Minister Abe indicated he would decide whether the government should raise the consumption tax rate based on the GDP outcome for this period. A November 2014 survey of the Japan Center for Economic Research estimated that the government's first preliminary GDP growth estimate for the third quarter of 2014 would be 2.47%. However, the actual estimate was far worse than economists expected, pegging third quarter GDP growth at negative 1.6%. Independent forecast errors rose to about 4 percentage points in this period. Moreover, for the government's second flash GDP estimate, most economists expected an upward revision, but GDP growth was in fact revised downward. In April 2014, the consumption tax rate increased from 5 to 8%, and economists have become worried about business conditions after the tax hike.

The media have criticized the poor performance of economic forecasts. In the behavioral economics literature, some researchers argue that economic forecasting is not rational. Yamasawa (2011) summarized the various kinds of economic forecaster bias, such as herding and wishful expectations.

On the other hand, Iizuka (2014) argues that poor forecast performance is to at least some extent caused by the Statistics Bureau. According to Iizuka, at the time of the first preliminary estimate, forecasters do not know the material inventory and supply chain inventory statistics for that quarter. When it comes to the second preliminary estimate, the breakdown of estimate results of the demand side and the supply side are not open to the public. Thus, one cause of the forecast error is insufficient public information.

3.5. Monthly GDP

To know what Statistics Bureau's QE of the GDP will be ahead of time, several institutes calculate the monthly GDP before the QE for that quarter is released. The "monthly GDP" is quarterly GDP data that has been converted to monthly figures. Most basic GDP statistics, such as consumption and capital investment statistics, are calculated based on monthly data from sources like the Index of Industrial Production and trade statistics. Monthly GDP data provide information on business cycles. It is important that monthly GDP data is available to academic researchers, as researchers use this data to perform a variety of empirical studies.

One method to obtain monthly GDP is the bridge equation mentioned in Section 2.3. Equation (1) is estimated quarterly. If this relationship holds on a monthly basis, we can estimate monthly GDP series. We can obtain the monthly Q_t, by substituting monthly M_t into the equation rather than quarterly M_t.

The Japan Center for Economic Research has released monthly GDP data since January 1999. In addition, the NLI Research Institute began to release monthly GDP data from almost the same period. For more information about the methodology that the Japan Center for Economic Research uses to calculate monthly GDP, see Yamasawa (2003).

The Cabinet Office does not release monthly GDP data, but it does release integrated Private Consumption estimates on a monthly basis. These estimates are the monthly index of consumption, which is the largest component of GDP.

Hara and Yamane (2013) introduced another model for estimating monthly GDP using the bridge equation. They set quarterly GDP as a dependent variable and set the levels of the Index of Industrial Production and Index of Tertiary Industries Activity as the explanatory variables in their bridge equation. They also added data reduced to principal components to their explanatory variables, and attempted to fit various time series into their equation to create a new method of estimating monthly GDP.

It is appropriate that monthly GDP is not considered to be a forecast of GDP but rather is considered to be new real GDP data. Monthly GDP enable us to analyze the economic outlook in detail. For academic use, it can be a proxy for the overall economy. Monthly GDP data is desirable in empirical econometric studies because it gives analysts a larger sample size to work with, which improves the accuracy of estimations. In the past, analysts had to analyze monthly data from sources such as the Index of Industrial Production when analyzing production output, but if monthly GDP data becomes readily available, analysts can use it instead to make more detailed analyses.

However, monthly GDP fluctuates too much for analysis by growth rate. For this, it is better to use the real GDP gap, which is the difference between actual GDP and potential GDP (Yamasawa, 2003).

4. Nowcasting and the Dynamic Factor Model

4.1. Nowcasting

Recently, the concept of "nowcasting" — a portmanteau combination of "now" and "forecasting" — is spreading. According to Banbura *et al.* (2013), nowcasting means forecasting for the very near future or the very recent past. The word originates in meteorology. On the website of the Japanese Meteorological Agency, for example, a nowcasting page enables viewers to access approximately 1-hour forecasts for rain, tornados, and thunder.

"Nowcasting" is easy to understand if it is compared to earthquake forecasts. Ordinary economic forecasts are forecasts of "earthquakes that have not happened yet", but nowcasting is a method of capturing "earthquakes that have happened already" as quickly as possible.

An example of nowcasting is given on the "nowcasting" website of the Federal Reserve Bank of Cleveland (Figure 3). This site displays the inflation rate "nowcast" of the current month, and updates this data daily. For example, it displayed the December 2014 inflation rate of the consumer price index in that same month, and provided daily updates.

According to the *International Journal of Forecasting,* which focused on nowcasting in 2013 (volume 29), many central banks around the world

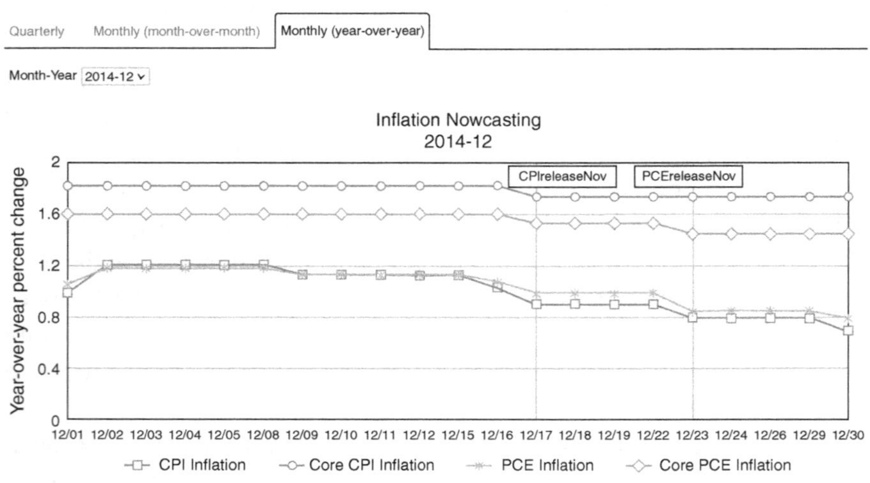

Figure 3. Inflation nowcasting

Source: Federal Reserve Bank of Cleveland (https://www.clevelandfed.org/)

attempt to nowcast. Nowcasting has the same characteristics as QE forecasts in that both methods involve forecasting quarterly GDP. However, unlike QE forecasting, nowcasting involves gathering a large amount of data and updating forecasts when actual data are updated. Another point of difference is that nowcasting is mainly carried out using state space and factor models.

Nowcasting has become popular in the business world. "Nowcast.com" was established in 2011 in London to provide GDP forecasts of many countries, founded by Domenico Giannone and Lucrezia Reichlin, two pioneer researchers in the field.

The SWIFT Index is an index of GDP nowcasting of OECD countries. Named after the Society for Worldwide Interbank Financial Telecommunication (SWIFT), an organization formed in 1973 in Brussels and supported by financial institutions, the index provides nowcasting of the GDPs of the United States, the United Kingdom, Germany, and other OECD countries. It uses financial trade volumes to estimate GDP.

4.2. Dynamic factor model

In the methodology of nowcasting, the dynamic factor model is the most common method used to perform nowcasting. This section explains this model.

The dynamic factor model is expressed in the form of the state space model.

The state space model includes state variables that cannot be observed. Using this method, we incorporate quarterly GDP data from the Index of Industrial Production as the observable variables, and "business cycle" data series, for example, as unobservable variables. This is the dynamic factor.

In this method, the vector X_t is made up of n observable items, and the vector F_t is made up of q state variables. If we assume that F_t is decided by F_{t-1}, the state space model can be arranged as follows:

$$X_t = \mu + \Lambda F_t + e_t \text{ (observation equation)}$$

$$F_t = \mu + \mathrm{A} F_{t-1} + \mathrm{B} u_t \text{ (state equation)},$$

where e_t and u_t are error terms.

The merit of this model is that the number of time-series data is not constrained. We can integrate many series into one dynamic factor, and this dynamic factor gives an insight into business conditions.

A typical example of a dynamic factor model that analyses the business cycle is the Stock–Watson model, which assumes an unobservable variable that indicates "business conditions". The movement of this unobservable variable is restricted by the state equation. In addition, the variables that express the business cycle in the Stock–Watson model are reflected in observable series, such as the Index of Industrial Production and the unemployment rate. The model develops one business condition index by integrating many monthly time series.

If we adopt the state equation, the business condition is expressed by F_t, although in the Stock–Watson model it is not a vector but rather a variable. In the observation equation X_t, a number of regression variables, including the Index of Industrial Production, the effective job openings-to-applications ratio, and large electric companies' power consumption statistics, are considered to be a single vector.

The Nikkei BI is a Stock–Watson-type index (Figure 4). It has been released since June 2000 on a monthly basis by the Nikkei Inc. (literally the "Japan Economic Newspaper"). The BI estimates business

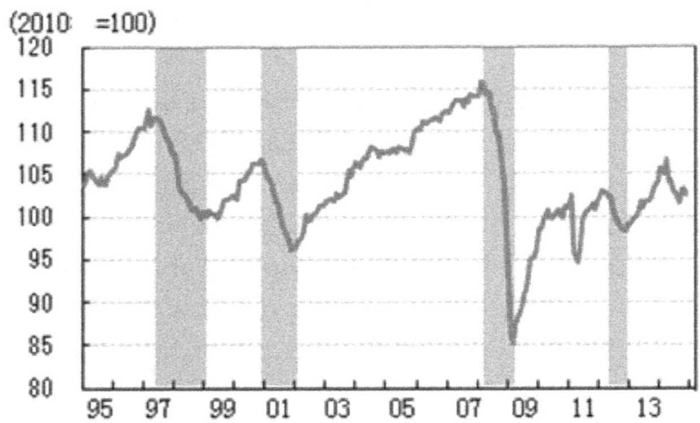

Figure 4. Nikkei business index

Source: *Nihon Keizai Shimbun* website (http://www.nikkei.com/)

conditions based on the Index of Industrial Production, retail and wholesale sales, extra labor hours, and the effective job openings-to-applications ratio.

4.3. State space model of monthly GDP

Mariano and Murasawa (2010) extended the dynamic factor model and developed monthly GDP forecasts using the state space model.

The following is the state space model again:

$$X_t = \mu + \Lambda F_t + e_t \text{ (observation equation)}$$

$$F_t = \mu + \mathrm{A}F_{t-1} + \mathrm{B}u_t \text{ (state equation),}$$

where e_t and u_t are error terms.

X_t is a vector of n observable variables. Most of these are monthly datasets, such as the Index of Industrial Production, but quarterly GDP is also included as a variable. This variable appears once a quarter but is missing for the rest of the period.

The relationship of quarterly GDP (seasonally adjusted) with monthly GDP (seasonally adjusted) is as follows:

GDP in April–June quarter = average of monthly GDP in April, May, and June.

In the Stock–Watson model, F_t is a singular variable that indexes business conditions, but here, F_t is monthly GDP. The basic consideration is that if the "business conditions" figure represents the movement of the economy, then it is identical to real monthly GDP. Therefore, the state equation should be constructed by setting one state variable that expresses "business conditions" as the monthly GDP.

The state space model can be solved by optimizing the likelihood function, but this includes-missing data as quarterly GDP data is only observable once every 3 months. However, the coefficient parameters can be estimated by adopting an Expectation-Maximization (EM) algorithm, which makes the missing data zero, and then inserts random data with a mean of zero and a distribution of 1 into the equation. This method has been taken on by recent nowcasting analyses.

4.4. Applications of the dynamic factor model

In recent nowcasting analyses, applying an extended version of the dynamic factor model has become popular. In the Stock–Watson model and the state space expression of monthly GDP, only one dynamic factor can be used. However, this is not the case in all equations. The observation equation in the state space model indicates that n observable variables are explained by q dynamic factors. If $q = 1$, this is a model of one dynamic factor, and if q is greater than one, it is a model of multiple dynamic factors.

The dynamic factor model allows for a variety of time series to be used as the observable variable X_t. Some researchers have attempted to use financial indicators, such as stock prices and interest rates as their observable variable, while others have attempted to use survey data about business conditions.

Furthermore, real-time updates have become popular in the nowcasting field recently. These update the forecasts immediately by incorporating new data into the equation as it is released. For example, after the release of the Index of Industrial Production, such updates estimate GDP immediately.

When real-time updates are included in the dynamic factor model, some actual data goes missing as new data has a different time frame to old data. A commonly-used solution to this problem is to fill the missing data using the Kalman filter.

5. Expansion of the Forecast Field

5.1. From monthly to daily data

One possible future research trend could be the use of higher frequency data. Modern forecasters are shifting their focus to forecasting monthly data rather than quarterly data, and daily data rather than monthly data. Financial data, such as interest rates and stock market data, are easily obtained daily data, and several researchers use this daily financial data to measure business conditions.

Some researchers are also utilizing sales data. The Nikkei Inc. has stored point of sales (POS) data and analyzed these data for 20 years.

The University of Tokyo (TU) Daily Price Index uses POS data as a price index. The TU daily price Index project is led by Tsutomu Watanabe of Tokyo University. TU's index calculates the daily price index using supermarket price and sales data stored on the POS system. The index covers 300 stores and more than 200,000 items. Daily series are released 3 days after the relevant period. There are a number of ways of integrating large volumes of price data, but TU's system adapts the Törnqvist index, which is a kind of weighted average method that considers both price and sales (Watanabe and Watanabe, 2014).

The TU daily price index gained the public's attention when it captured price movements better than the official monthly consumer price index (CPI) after the Great East Japan Earthquake. In addition, it allowed researchers to obtain price information faster than previously when the consumption tax rate was raised from 5–8% in April 2014 (Figure 5).

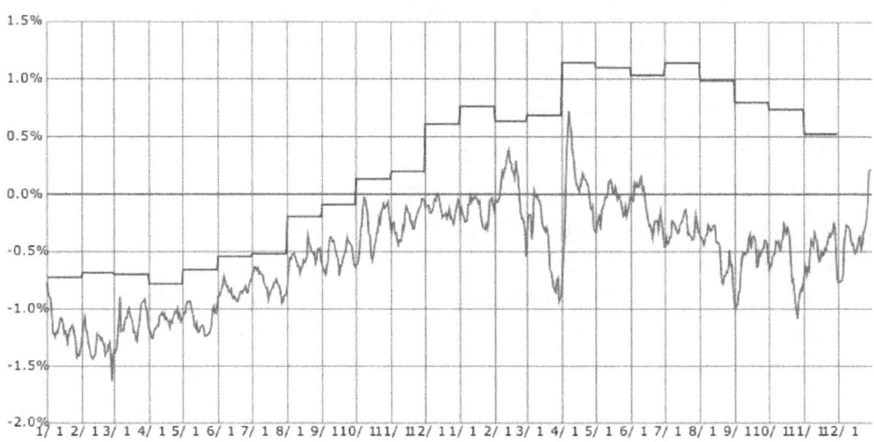

Figure 5. University of Tokyo daily price index

Note: Bottom line is the TU Daily Price Index, top line is the official Consumer Price Index
Source: TU Daily Price Project (http://www.cmdlab.co.jp/price_u-tokyo/media_e)

The weak point of this index is that it cannot cover all the items of the CPI. The official CPI is calculated using the prices of all the items that consumers purchase, so the weight of goods and services is each about 50%. However, the TU daily price index mainly covers daily goods sold by convenience stores and supermarkets, meaning that it doesn't properly represent consumption trends as a whole.

A common weakness of high-frequency data is that they tend to fluctuate substantially, which makes it difficult for analysts to establish basic trends using this data. Thus, the development of a statistical method to grasp these basic economic trends is necessary.

The TU project team's experimental development of a daily sales data index proves that forecasting daily movements of this data is possible. Converting annual GDP data into daily data is difficult at present, but if consumption data is recorded in real time in the future, forecasting the GDP daily will become a real possibility.

5.2. Using search engines

One form of high-frequency data that analysts can obtain is "big data". Choi and Varian (2012) explain how to use Google Trends and apply it to forecasting. Google Trends has provided daily and weekly reports on volumes of queries since 2004. It allows users to view graphs displaying the volume of any search term and download this data as a comma-separated value (CSV) file for free.

Choi and Varian (2012) introduced several studies that attempted to use the volumes of search engine queries related to certain GDP statistics to ascertain the movement of those statistics. These studies looked into, for example, auto sales, unemployment rates, tourism data, and consumer confidence index trends as indicated by Google search volumes.

Another example of business cycle analysis using search engines is a project by Yahoo! Japan, called "Is it possible to capture the 'present' business condition? (http://event.yahoo.co.jp/bigdata/keiki/)", first announced on the Yahoo! Japan homepage on April 13, 2013. This project investigated the correlation between actual business conditions and volumes of queries related to those business conditions. It also attempted to forecast a diffusion index of economic indicators based on related search volumes. The study showed that the population of search terms input into Yahoo! Japan in 2012 was 7.5 billion, with about 600,000 of these terms used regularly, and 206 of the terms related to business conditions. Yahoo! Japan grouped terms with similar meanings and integrated them into one series using principal component analysis. It then regressed this principal component into the diffusion index to estimate GDP data. While the firm has not provided a recent update of these forecasts, the method represents one way of forecasting business conditions using search term data.

Shiroki *et al.* (2013), researchers from the Bank of Japan, tried to apply Google Trends to nowcasting by investigating the correlation between tourism sales before and after the Great East Japan Earthquake and trends in tourism-related search terms. They concluded that volumes of queries contained useful information for tourism sales.

5.3. Application to regional statistics

Several researchers have attempted to use nowcasting to estimate Gross Regional Product (GRP), to give the production output of each prefecture in Japan. The economic activity of prefectures can be ascertained from the Cabinet Office's prefectural GRP statistics, but the government takes a long time to release these data. In fact, the government releases GRP data for Japan's 47 prefectures 2 years and 3 months after the relevant period. As of March 2015, we have only annual GRP data for 2011 for the 47 prefectures.

Recently, examining business conditions by region has become very important because different regions have divergent business conditions. Many prefectures compile their own diffusion indexes of local business conditions, integrating various economic series. However, few prefectures have attempted to make flash estimates of their GRP, which is a better indicator than a diffusion index in terms of comprehensiveness.

Hyogo prefecture releases QE of its GRP (Ashiya, 2009). QE are flash estimates using a method that is also applied to national statistics. Using the least squares method, Ashiya (2009) estimated quarterly series by fewer indicators than those used for the final estimates. For example, Ashiya estimated final private consumption using the household survey, retail and wholesale sales, and department store sales data.

Gunma Prefectural Office (2006) estimates the GRP of Gunma prefecture. A unique aspect of their estimate is that it is a supply-side estimation, while flash GDP estimates is usually made using the demand side.

Yoshihisa Inada developed a method to estimate the GRP of Osaka prefecture. This estimate uses principal component analysis, the forecast series can be released faster than government data, and it has demonstrated accuracy (Ogawa and Inada, 2013).

The Cabinet Office also publishes monthly expenditure statistics for each prefecture called the Regional Domestic Expenditure Index (RDEI). These statistics give several components of GRP, such as private final consumption, private residential investment, private equipment investment, and public investment. We can estimate monthly GRP by estimating the rest of the GDP expenditure components. Yamasawa (2014) estimated final public consumption and net exports for 47 prefectures using panel data estimation. This monthly real GRP for 47 prefectures can be used to analyze business conditions (Figure 6).

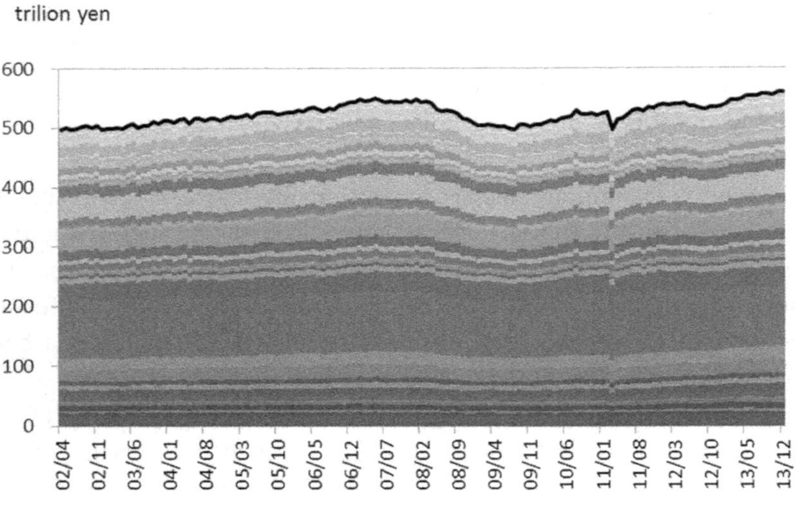

Figure 6. Real monthly GRP (accumulation of 47 prefectures)

Source: Yamasawa (2014)

Real monthly prefectural GRP can be forecast at about the same rate as the quarterly GDP is forecast. If researchers had access to this monthly prefectural data, they would be able to use it in a variety of econometric studies. For this reason, it is important that a more comprehensive and timely method of forecasting the GRP for each of Japan's prefectures be developed.

References

Ashiya, Tunenori (2009) "Present Conditions and Problems of Prefectural Accounting," *Statistics*, 96, pp. 54–71 (in Japanese).

Banbura, Marta, Giannone, Domenico, Modugno, Michele and Reichlin, Lucrezia (2013) "Nowcasting and the Real-time Data Flow," ECB Working Paper, No. 1564.

Choi, Hyunyoung and Varian, Hal (2012) "Predicting the Present with Google Trends," *The Economic Record*, 88, pp. 2–9.

Gunma Prefectural Office (2006) "Practices and Problems of New Quarterly Preliminary Estimate of Prefectural Economic Account — Supply Side Approach," National Account Quarterly No. 132, Economic and Social Research Institute, Cabinet Office (in Japanese).

Hara, Naoko and Yamane, Shotaro (2013) "New Monthly Estimation Approach for Nowcasting GDP Growth: The Case of Japan," Bank of Japan Working Paper Series No. 13-E-14.

Iizuka, Nobuo (2014) "Making Hasty Information Disclosure of GDP Preliminary Estimates," Keizai Kyositsu, *Nihon Keizai Shimbun*, Morning Edition, December 26 (in Japanese).

Inada, Yoshihisa (2013) "Super Short-Term Forecasting for Judging Business Conditions," Keizai Kyousitsu, Nikkei Inc., Morning Edition, September 20 (in Japanese).

Kawagoe, Masaaki (2007) "A Consideration of Revision of the Growth Rate — Analysis of Real-Time Data of Real GDP," National Account Quarterly No. 134, Economic and Social Research Institute, Cabinet Office (in Japanese).

Komaki, Yasuyuki (2005) "Measurement Errors or Forecast Errors: An Analysis of GDP Revision," *Kokumin Keizai Zasshi*, 191(1), pp. 1–15, Kobe University (in Japanese).

Komine, Takao (2005) "Introduction to the New Business Cycle Observation," Nihon Hyoron Sha (in Japanese).

Mankiw, N. Gregory and Shapiro, Matthew D. (1986) "News or Noise: An Analysis of GNP Revisions." *Survey of Current Business*, pp. 20–25.

Mariano, S. Roberto and Murasawa, Yasutomo (2010) "A Coincident Index, Common Factors, and Monthly Real GDP," *Oxford Bulletin of Economics and Statistics*, 72(1), pp. 27–46.

Ogawa, Ryo and Inada, Yoshihisa (2013) "The Development of Preliminary Estimates of Prefectural GDP that are Consistent, Quick, and Accurate," APIR Discussion Paper Series No. 33 2013/4 (in Japanese).

Saito, Taro (2012) "An Inspection of the Accuracy of Forecasts of Preliminary GDP Estimates," Weekly Economist Letter, NLI Research Institute, May 11, (in Japanese).

Shiroki, Noriyuki, Matsumura, Kohei, and Matsumoto, Azusa (2013) "An Availability of Search Term Data to Judge Business Conditions," BOJ Reports & Research Papers, January (in Japanese).

Tsutomu, Watanabe and Kota, Watanabe (2014) "Estimating Daily Inflation Using Scanner Data: A Progress Report," CARF Working Paper Series, CARF-F-342, February.

Yamasawa, Nariyasu (2003) "Monthly GDP as a Business Condition Indicator," in Asako, Kazumi, and Fukuda, Shinichi (eds.) "*Business Cycles and Business Forecasts*," Tokyo University Press, pp. 201–231 (in Japanese).

Yamasawa, Nariyasu (2011) "New Essays on Economic Forecasts," *Nihon Hyoron Shya* (in Japanese).

Yamasawa, Nariyasu (2014) "Measuring the Indirect Losses from Natural Disasters: The Case of the Great East Japan Earthquake," *61st Annual North American Meetings of the Regional Science Association International*, Washington.

Chapter 2

The Development of the Japanese CQM and Examples of Its Dynamic Applications

Yoshihisa Inada

Konan University and the Asia Pacific Institute of Research

1. Introduction

In Chapter 1, we explained the estimation methods of flash data, carried out high-frequency forecasts, and surveyed the development of those forecasts. In this chapter and in Chapter 3, we will show sample current quarter model (CQM) forecasts of the Japanese and US economies using high-frequency forecast methods such as the bridge equation and the principal component analysis forecast models. Drawing on many years of forecast experience, we will also evaluate the effectiveness of the CQM.[1] The first half of this chapter will introduce the applications of CQM forecasts on the Japanese economy and analyze the accuracy of the technique. The second half will introduce a recent example that demonstrates how the model can be used effectively. This chapter will also present an

[1] In this report, I refer to generic models with a high-forecast frequency as "high-frequency forecast models", however some researchers call these models "nowcasting" models. I call the specific model that is being developed in Chapters 2 and 3 the "CQM Forecast".

example application of the CQM forecast technique in which we perform preliminary estimates of Japan's prefectural GDPs. Through this analysis, we will demonstrate that the CQM is an effective method for informing political policymaking and business decisions.

2. The Applications of CQM Forecasts on the Japanese Economy

In the past, macroeconometric models played an important role in economic forecasting, as well as in drafting and analyzing the effects of economic policy. However, after the 1970s oil crisis, the accuracy of those models came under question, and economists started debating the effectiveness of those models, testing whether time series analysis models were more accurate than structural models. However, demand for economic forecasts did not decrease, and in fact analysts started forecasts more frequently. What's more, companies started issuing financial reports quarterly instead of annually or half-yearly, and market forecasts and revisions took on an important role in companies' decision-making processes. As the business environment changing and demand for a more accurate, higher frequency forecast method increasing, Professor Emeritus L. R. Klein of University of Pennsylvania developed a technique that answered this demand: Current quarter model (CQM) forecasts. Professor Klein and other economists developed this model in the late 1980s and put it into practice in the early 1990s (see further Klein and Sojo (1989), Klein and Park (1993), and Klein and Park (1995).

Since 1993, we have applied Klein's technique and carried out CQM forecasts of the Japanese economy on a weekly basis. These forecasts have confirmed that the model is highly accurate, and they have increased the accuracy of short-term quarterly macroeconometric model forecasts combining with CQM forecasts.[2] Since the 1990s, the CQM has led the way in facilitating high-frequency model forecasts and also in complementing short-term forecasts.

The CQM is unique in that it makes use of monthly flash data by regularly including its changes into forecasts, such as its quarterly GDP

[2]For example, the Asia Pacific Institute of Research has since 2005 combined the CQM into its quarterly macroeconometric model forecasts to improve the accuracy of those forecasts.

forecasts. The model determines the statistical relationship between monthly data and quarterly national income statistics (showing GDP and its structural components), producing flexible forecasts. This model was created to make forecasts based solely on econometric methods, and it does not allow the analyst to make any individual adjustments to the forecasts. As a rule, the model calculates using monthly data as it is released and makes forecasts using a weekly base, adjusting its forecast for either the current month or the subsequent month as it goes. There is no other model that produces forecasts of the Japanese economy to this frequency. Thanks to the frequency of its forecasts, the model is able to produce actual figures and trends that forecast the immediate movements of the Japanese economy.

In general terms, to create an accurate forecast, you need (1) to use an exacting and stable model, and (2) to set the initial conditions correctly. The latter step is particularly important when your model is nonlinear.

As is well known, GDP statistics are secondary data that have been calculated using monthly data as the base statistic. The Department of National Accounts, Economic and Social Research Institute, Cabinet Office of Japan (2012) follows a set manual to calculate quick estimates (QE) of the GDP on a quarterly basis. If we follow the Department's method, we can use basic monthly indicator variables to generate QE. The Government's estimation method, which is a stable, exacting model, is included in the CQM.

The next task we should consider is the task of setting the initial conditions correctly. The basic monthly indicator variable used in the CQM to find the GDP is estimated using the autoregressive integrated moving average (ARIMA) time series model, and as new monthly data is slotted into this model a week after it is announced, the model consistently maintains its up-to-date and correct initial conditions.

We will explain the CQM's forecast process using one of its approaches, the expenditure-side approach, as an example. CQM forecasts are made in the following four steps (see, Inada (2009)):

(1) Prior processing of monthly indicator variables

Firstly, we must select the data to be used in the model (which will be the basis for our GDP estimation) and perform a unit root test of that data.

Next, to make the data stationary, we will apply the filtering process and make first differences. Note that in the Japanese CQM, over 50 sources of monthly indicator variables are used.

(2) Time series (ARIMA) model calculations using monthly indicator variables and two quarter projection forecasts: Setting correct initial conditions

In this step, we make the data that represents components of the GDP stationary and use that data (y_t) in our time series model estimations:

$$y_t = \alpha_1 y_{t-1} + \alpha_2 y_{t-2} + \cdots + \varepsilon_t, \qquad \text{where } \varepsilon_t\text{: error term.}$$

Next, we select the optimal model order and carry out our half-year projection forecast. The time series model's forecast performance is considered to be suitable for making forecasts over a 6 month period. By changing this 6 month forecast figure into quarterly figures, we can generate two-quarter forecasts of basic GDP data.

(3) Calculating basic quarterly data and GDP expenditure using bridge equations: Estimating with an exact, stable model

Let's examine a simple example of this process by looking at how to calculate private residential investment. According to the QE estimation manual, private residential investment is calculated by adjusting progressive weight to the planned dwelling construction expenditure. Here, we turn the net planned (residential) construction expenditure, which is our basic monthly indicator variable, into quarterly data and use it as an explanatory variable to regress private residential investment. This regression equation is called a "bridge equation". Ordinarily, if there is one basic monthly indicator variable for estimating a component of the GDP, the explanatory variable's coefficient will be close to 1. Note that variables take the first difference (DIFF). All of the expenditure components of the GDP released in the QE are estimated using bridge equations. The monthly indicator variables used in bridge equations to estimate GDP components are shown in Table 1.

DIFF (JP_IFR) = f (DIFF (w_i*ΣICVDW/PCDWELL00))
JP_IFR: Private residential investment in real term
w_i: Progressive weight, ICVDW: net planned (residential) construction expense
PCDWELL00: Construction costs deflator

Table 1. Data used in bridge equations

Component of GDP	Related monthly indicator variable	Related monthly deflator data
Household consumption	Integrated consumption index, overall consumer price index (CPI), retail sales, new car sales, floor area of housing starts	CPI (goods and services), CPI (automotive, house rent, overall)
Government expenditure	Indices of government services	CPI (services)
Private residential investment	Planned private dwelling construction expenditure	Construction costs deflator (housing)
Private non-residential investment	Information service industry sales, private machinery orders, integrated construction statistics (non-residential), capital goods shipment index	Corporate service price index (software), input price index (electrical machinery), corporate goods price index (capital)
Public investment	Integrated construction statistics (public works)	Infrastructure construction costs deflator (public works)
Changes in private inventory	Industrial inventory index, industrial inventory index (final demand)	Domestic corporate goods price index
Changes in public inventory	Changes in expenses for foodstuffs control	Domestic corporate goods price index
Export of goods and services	Customs clearance statistics (exports), balance of payments (shipment, travel, and other service payments received)	Export price index, CPI (overall)
Foreign income received	Balance of payments (income received)	Domestic corporate goods price index, CPI, export price index
Import of goods and services	Customs clearance statistics (imports), balance of international payments (shipment, travel, and other service payments made)	Export price index, CPI (overall)
Foreign income paid	Balance of payments (income paid)	Domestic corporate goods price index, CPI, export price index
Compensation of employee	Total cash earnings, employment figures	—

(4) Using bridge equations to make CQM forecasts for the upcoming two quarters

By substituting the two-quarter forecast value for basic GDP data found in Step 2 as an explanatory variable into the bridge equations for the estimated expenditure component of the GDP, we can generate our GDP forecast value. This value is the total of half-yearly expenditure and the other components of the GDP.

Step 1 is carried out quarterly, but Steps 2–4 are repeated using roll-over data weekly. This means that we can insert new information of basic monthly data for estimating GDP into our weekly forecast updates. In general, as we obtain new data, the accuracy of our GDP forecasts also increases. We repeat this process until the current quarter's QE is announced. The CQM's GDP forecasts therefore change every week, rather than just once a quarter. By examining the changes in the forecast value on a weekly basis, we can make a reasonable decision about which direction the economy is moving in on a weekly basis. This is why the information that the CQM provides is valuable for not only market economists and traders but also political policymakers.

3. GDP Statistics and Forecast Models

Table 2 shows the three sides of the GDP and how frequently these figures are announced in Japan and the US. As the table shows, figures for these three sides of the GDP are not necessarily released on a quarterly basis. The Japanese and US governments only release expenditure and distribution data on a quarterly basis. However, in Japan's case, only employee compensation data is released on a quarterly basis. Japan's other distribution data is released only once a year. Both Japan and the US's GDP production data is not released quarterly. The expenditure side of the GDP is released in Japan in two stages of preliminary estimates, whereas in the US, it is released in three: advance, preliminary, and final.

Monthly data related to GDP expenditure, distribution, and production are not estimated in Japan. In the US, private consumption and capital investment data are estimated monthly, and they form the basis for the quarterly GDP data. Data on certain components of the distribution GDP, such as household income, is also released monthly by the US.

Table 2. Frequency of official announcements of national income statistics

		Monthly	Quarterly	Yearly
Expenditure side GDP	Japan	×	✓	✓
	US	✓ (in part)	✓	✓
Production side GDP	Japan	×	×	✓
	US	×	×	✓
Distribution side GDP	Japan	×	✓ (in part)	✓
	US	✓ (in part)	✓	✓

In his US CQM approach, Klein presents three approaches to estimate the GDP:

1. The expenditure-side approach
2. The distribution-side approach
3. The production-side approach

Klein argues that the ideal (forecast) GDP growth rate should be an average of the growth rates forecasted by these three models (Klein and Park (1993) and (1995).

Expenditure-side approach

GDP = C (consumption) + I (investment) + G (government spending) + E (exports) – M (Imports).

Distribution-side approach

GDP = W (wages) + YF (corporate profits) + IN (interest) + R (rents) + TI (indirect business taxes) – S (subsidies).

Production-side approach

GDP = GP (gross production) – IP (intermediate production) = VA (value added).

Naturally, it is recommended that the three approaches used to determine the GDP in the three-side equivalence principle are used in a GDP forecast model, but in the CQM, we decide on the approaches that we ultimately use depending on how frequently GDP data is released.

In a forecast model that employs the first two approaches, we use a bridge equation that brings together monthly indicator variable data and the individual components of the quarterly GDP estimates. We cannot make forecasts using the third approach, the production-side approach, as production data are not fit to be used on a quarterly basis. This is because production GDP data (value added) are only released annually. However, by treating the quarterly gross domestic expenditures (GDE) from the three-side equivalence principle as equal to the GDP, we are able to input monthly production data into the principal component analysis forecast model and use it to forecast real GDP and the GDP inflator, our variable set.

As a result, the US CQM forecasts are carried out by using three approaches: (1) the expenditure-side approach, (2) the distribution-side approach, and (3) the production-side approach.[3] Conversely, the Japanese CQM forecasts are carried out using the expenditure-side approach centrally, while the distribution-side approach is not used. The Japanese government does release quarterly figures for distribution components of the Japanese GDP, but only once a year. The only distribution figures the government releases quarterly in the QE are employee compensation figures. It is because of these restrictions that we do not employ the distribution-side approach when making CQM forecasts about the Japanese economy. Instead, we employ the principal component analysis forecast model just as we would when making CQM forecasts of the US economy, using the method to estimate the real GDP and the GDP deflator (Inada (2007)).

In the principal component analysis model, we use 15 representative monthly variables to calculate the main component of the real GDP, and six variables in the main component calculation of the GDP deflator. The 15 monthly variables used in the calculation of the main component of the real GDP are as follows:

1. Industrial production index
2. Industrial inventory index

---

[3] In the Kumasaka model, unlike in the Klein model, forecasts are made using (1) the expenditure side model, (2) the distribution side model, and (3) an average of both models' results.

3. Real household final consumption expenditure (HFCE)
4. Real retail sales
5. Real planed dwelling construction expenses
6. Real private machinery orders
7. Real public construction expenditure
8. Export volume
9. Import volume
10. Employed population
11. Ratio of job offers to applications (the "active opening rate")
12. Real average monthly cash earning
13. Terms of trade
14. Exchange rate
15. Spread of long- and short-term interest rates.

The six variables used in the main component calculation of the GDP deflator are:

1. National consumer price index (overall)
2. Domestic corporate goods price index
3. Construction cost deflator (housing)
4. Construction cost deflator (public works)
5. Import price index
6. Average net monthly salary.

We change these monthly variables into quarterly figures and calculate the principal component based on these figures. We then regress the real GDP and the GDP deflator on these main components directly. Bridge equations, which explain the real GDP and the GDP deflator by principal components, have been chosen as the most suitable model for doing this.

To see another example of this technique's application, turn to Section 5, where the principal component analysis model is used to forecast GRPs.

4. Consensus vs. the CQM: A Provisional Conclusion about the Value of the Two Techniques

Inada (2011) has compared in detail the forecast accuracy of the CQM and market consensus estimates (provided by the Japan Center for Economic

Research's ESP forecast survey). Through this comparison, Inada came to the following provisional conclusions:

(1) Although market consensus forecasts are an average of individual forecasters' estimates, the accuracy of the method was surprisingly high. In reality, the performance of market consensus was comparative to that of the CQM.
(2) In terms of the movement of individual forecasts, consensus forecasts were extremely stable and rarely changed. This meant that it was difficult to tell from consensus forecasts when changes in the economy occurred.
(3) In comparison, the movements of CQM forecasts were dynamic, so it could be used to obtain basic monthly data about the GDP. The method's dynamism also made its forecasts more accurate. Inada found that in addition to CQM's accurate forecasts, it made them 2 months ahead of market consensus estimates.
(4) As Inada showed using a number of examples, consensus forecasts were stable, but were affected by market sentiment.
(5) Inada concluded by determining that the CQM was an effective model as it was subjective and data-dependent.

5. The Usefulness of the CQM: Disputing the Effects of the Rise in the Consumption Tax

Within the provisional conclusions Inada make about the CQM in the previous section, points (3) and (4) are key points of interest because when companies and governments make important decisions, they require correct and subjective forecasts of the short-term movements of the economy.

In April 2014, the Japanese Government raised the consumption from 5–8%. The Government had also decided to raise the tax again from 8–10% in October 2015. However, in July 2014, 3 months after the first round of tax hikes, media outlets were optimistically reporting that the slump caused by the tax hike had not been as severe as had been predicted. The prevailing sentiment was that a second tax hike would be a reasonable step. The last time the government raised taxes in April 1997, it raised them by two percentage points, but in 2014, it raised them by three. In real terms, the slump that the market suffered from as a result of the 2014 tax hike was worse than the slump that occurred after the 1997 tax hike. The reason why consumers and businesses viewed the tax hike favorably this time around is because the first two "arrows" of Abenomics (the large-scale stock price increase and the significant weakening of the yen) had changed the way these groups thought about the economy (Figure 1). Additionally, in the autumn that followed the 1997 tax increase, Japan was threatened by the Asian Financial Crisis, but in 2014, the prevalent forecast was that the economy would not face any threats of that magnitude. Because of this, the media focused on the relatively standout statistics showing improvements that had been made after the downturn and speculated that the downturn from the 2014 was not as significant as the downturn that resulted from the 1997 tax hike, and that the country would recover from it sooner. However, forecasts from the data-dependent CQM cast doubt on the media's assertions. The following explanation of how the CQM can be used to dispel this kind of conjecture about the economy is based on an article that the author contributed to the *Keizai Kyoshitsu* (Economic Classroom) section of the July 22nd, 2014 Japanese edition of *The Nikkei* (called the *Nihon Keizai Shinbun*).

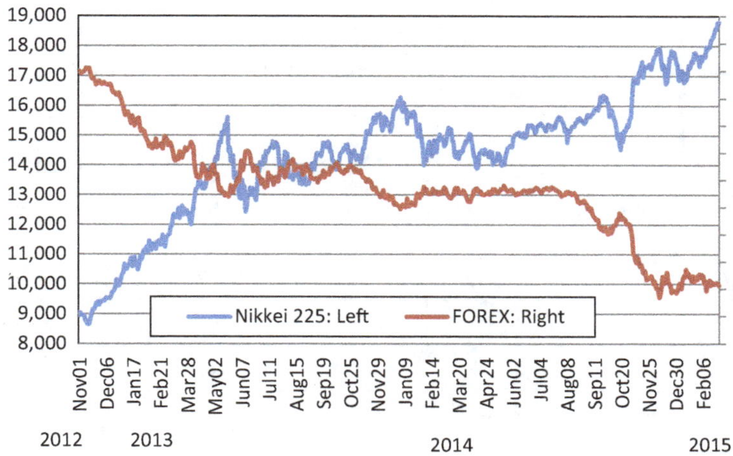

Figure 1. Stock prices and FOREX in the period of Abenomics

Data source: Nikkei Needs

This article was published over a month before August 13th, when the first round of preliminary GDP estimates for the April–June quarter would be released. On the 21st of July, the day before the article was published, about two-thirds of the basic monthly data required for estimating the April–June quarter GDP had been released. Following the CQM technique, the author forecast the unreleased June and July–September monthly data using a time series model, added this forecast data to the already announced April–May monthly data, then used a bridge equation to convert the data into GDP components, and finally forecast each component's real growth rate. Thanks to the CQM forecasts, the shape of the GDP in the April–June quarter had already become fairly apparent by this stage, and so the author was able to examine the movement of expenditure components of the GDP and make an appraisal of the state of the Japanese economy (see Figure 2).

The GDP has two main components: Domestic demand and net exports. The domestic demand component can be broken down further into private sector demand and public sector demand. Within private sector demand, the largest and most important component is private consumption. At the time, reports from news media outlets were expressing

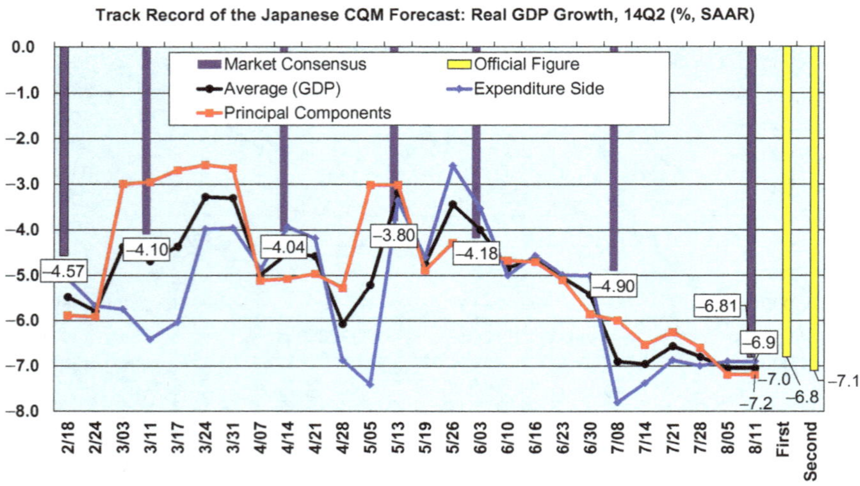

Figure 2. Track record of the Japanese CQM forecast of real GDP growth for the 2014 April–June quarter

sentiments like "department stores recovering, consumption stable" and "impact of the downturn lessening". These reports gave the public the impression that the effects that the downturn was having on consumer expenditure was comparatively weak.

However, we must be cautious about reports like these that compare current consumption statistics with the level that they were at in the same month of the previous year. As the months passed since April 2014, the size of the drop in demand from its level in 2013 did decrease, but this is not an appropriate measure of the size of the downturn. What these reports should have analyzed was how, excluding seasonal factors, the level of demand changed in the April–May period compared with the January–March quarter, when there was a late surge in spending prior to the tax hike.

Firstly, the seasonally adjusted Private Consumption Integrated Index, a comprehensive index of private consumption, tells us that private consumption in May 2014 rose by 1.3%, making a small recovery from large –8.1% drop in consumption recorded in April 2014. However, the average consumption level in the April–May period was 4.9% less than the average level in the January–March 2014 period. Moreover, the seasonally adjusted household consumption level for May, announced in the Family Income and Expenditure Survey, continued to fall, recording a –3.1% decrease from the April level. Average household consumption in April–May was 9.2% lower than the average level for January–March. The revised shipment index level for April–May announced in the Ministry of Economy, Trade and Industry's production statistics confirms that demand for durable consumer goods fell by 7.5% compared with the January–March average, while demand for non-durables fell by 5.3%, demonstrating that the downturn particularly affected durable goods. The real private consumption expenditure for the January–March quarter in 2014 did increase by 2.2% from the previous quarter, but this growth was consistent with the pre-tax hike growth in the January–March quarter in 1997. Durables in this period in 2014 performed three times better than they performed in the same period in 1997. On the other hand, service expenditure was lower in this period in 2014 than it was in 1997. This result demonstrates the impact of the unusually large snowfall that occurred in February 2014, which prevented consumers from leaving their houses. Because of this, we can say that there was a higher level of latent demand in the pre-tax hike period in 2014 than there was in 1997. All things considered, we forecast real private consumption expenditure in the April–June 2014 to drop by a fairly severe 4.2% from the previous quarter. This drop exceeded that of 3.5% in private consumption in the previous post-tax hike period in 1997.

For private residential investment forecast using the CQM, we make use of the planned dwelling construction expenditure figures (see Table 1). The average seasonally adjusted planned dwelling construction expenditure for the April–May 2014 period (author estimate) was 10.6% lower than the average expenditure for the January–March 2014 period. On the other hand, in the January–March quarter, new housing fell by 10.3% compared with the previous quarter, but real private residential investment rose by 3.1%. As the residential investment in GDP is estimated in progressive base, it followed that the downturn from the post-tax hike demand would hit full speed in the subsequent months. Based on this, the author forecasted that private residential investment would fall dramatically by 11.7% in the April–June quarter.

We use the capital goods shipment index when calculating private non-residential investment using the CQM (see Table 1). The average revised capital goods shipment index figure for the April–May period fell by the significant margin of 7.6% from its average level in January–March. However, as sales in the information service industry, which are related to software investment, were positive, the author forecast that the real private non-residential investment for the April–June quarter would only fall by 0.5% from the previous quarter.

As we have seen, the key components of private demand (private consumption, private residential investment, and private non-residential investment) were all falling in April–May 2014 compared to the previous quarter, making a large drop in the GDP that quarter inevitable.

But what about public sector demand? Let us examine the trends in the Government's capital investment. According to the "Integrated Statistics on Construction Works" issued by the Ministry of Land, Infrastructure and Transport, the May output of public works (seasonally adjusted, author estimate) rose by 5.3% from April, reaching positive figures for the first time in 6 months. Furthermore, the contract sum for public works in the April–June quarter rose by a substantial 26.3% from the previous quarter (seasonally adjusted). It should be noted, however, that the Integrated Statistics on Construction Works also reported that unused funds for public works continued to rise in May, up 25.7% from a year earlier. This indicates that an increase in the contract sum for public works does not immediately translate into an expansion in the construction industry. In the end, the real Government capital investment figure for the April–June 2014 quarter would rise by a measly 0.7% from the previous quarter.

The last figure to examine is the net exports figure. According to the trade statistics (preliminary reports), Japan's average (seasonally adjusted) trade deficit for April–May 2014 decreased by 41.9% from the January–March quarter. The CQM forecasted that the real export figure for the April–June quarter would rise by 0.8% from the previous quarter, but real imports would fall by 4.0%. It appeared that exports would make moderate gains, but imports would decrease as an aftereffect of the pre-tax hike demand. The end result was that the contribution of the growth rate of real net exports rose by 0.8 percentage points, the first time the growth rate had risen for four consecutive quarters.

We have now seen the most up-to-date forecasts of the April–June GDP and for individual GDP components. As Figure 2 shows, the July 21st expenditure-side CQM forecast, which is a total of all of the individual forecasts made above, had the real annualized growth at –6.9% (a 1.8% drop from the previous quarter). Meanwhile, the production-side forecast for annual growth was at –6.3%, and the average of the two was at –6.6%. The Market Consensus forecast of the real GDP growth rate released on July 10th (in the Japan Center for Economic Research's July ESP forecast survey) predicted a –4.9% drop, but this was an optimistic forecast compared with the most recent CQM forecast at the time. The CQM's monthly forecast track record was already forecasting that the growth rate would trend downwards from 4 to 7% well before market consensus.

The 6.9% negative growth on the expenditure side exceeded the 3.7% negative growth post-tax in the 1997 April–June quarter and indicated a loss similar to that experienced at the time of the Great East Japan Earthquake, when the growth rate also fell by 6.9%. The downturn, then, was more severe than had been initially predicted. A month before the first report for the April–June quarter GDP was released, the CQM was reporting that the effects of the consumption tax were not as mild as they were being portrayed in the media, and that the post-tax hike drop in consumption was particularly large. The actual first report, released 1 month later, estimated that the decrease in real annual GDP growth was 6.8%, which was exactly the same result as the CQM's final forecast.

Later, the first report on GDP growth for the July–September quarter (released on November 17th) announced that negative growth had continued from the previous quarter, estimating a 1.6% decrease in the growth rate. Taking this trend into account, the Government decided in late November to postpone the second tax hike planned for October 2015 until April 2017. The government's decision confirmed that the impact of the first consumption tax increase had indeed been great. This incident demonstrates just how useful the forecasts made by the CQM are.

6. Developments in the CQM: Preliminary GRP Estimates and National Developments

For local governments to develop effective policies, it is vital that they are aware of the scale of their local economy and the changes in its structure. The index that is most representative of this is each prefecture's gross regional product (GRP). A number of statistics are required to create the final GRP report, so its announcement usually takes between one and a half and 2 years. Currently, many local governments are creating policies and managing their finances without having an accurate grasp of the movements of their own region's economy.

Because of this, certain prefectures are performing preliminary estimates of their GRP, but only a limited number. One reason why many prefectures have yet to adopt preliminary estimates is because preliminary estimate levels often differ significantly from final report levels, and governments are concerned that this could create confusion when they are making judgments on the state of the economy (Ashiya (2009)). The problem with GRP estimates is that in the past, they have not been able to report speedily and accurately. To solve this problem, we present a GRP estimation method that uses principal component analysis. This method involves regressing time series data of GRP final report levels directly on preliminary statistics. However, the risk that comes with using this method is that it can create the macroeconomic problem of "multicollinearity", where coefficient estimates in a multiple regression change erratically in response to small changes in the model. An effective way of preventing this multicollinearity problem is to extract a number of vectors describing the components of the economy from preliminary statistics. In effect, this method involves mediating principal component analysis.

Ogawa and Inada (2013) tested the accuracy of this variation of the CQM method by using it to perform a preliminary estimate of the Osaka Prefecture GRP. They found that the method was an appropriate model for making estimations and that it produced accurate forecasts. In their summary, Ogawa and Inada anticipated that the method could be used to make accurate preliminary estimates of the GRPs of other prefectures. Encouraged by the results of this study, the Asia Pacific Institute of Research (APIR) started a project in which the Institute's analysts used the method to make preliminary estimates of the GRPs of the six prefectures that make up the Kansai region (Osaka, Hyogo, Kyoto, Shiga, Nara, and Wakayama Prefecture). In this project, APIR aimed to release 2- or 3-year forecasts of the movement of the Japanese and Kansai economies every quarter as the national GDP statistics are released. However, for the reasons already mentioned, APIR had to forecast a further 2 years of past data before forecasting the future movements of the Kansai GRP. To ensure that its estimates of future movements were believable, APIR needed to make highly accurate forecasts of its launch pad, the past 2 years of GRP movements. It was this practical need for both fast and accurate forecasts of the recent movements in the GRP that encouraged the analysts at APIR to start this project and adopt Ogawa and Inada's method. In Chapter 4, we will examine preliminary GRP estimation using the CQM in detail, while in Chapter 5, we will look into the developments of the CQM's application on a national level.

References

Ashiya, T. (2009) "Present Condition and Problems of Prefectural Accounting," Statistics No. 96, pp. 54–71 (in Japanese).

Economic and Social Research Institute (2012) "Estimation Method of Preliminary Quarterly GDP (QE)," Cabinet Office, Government of Japan.

Inada, Y. (2007) "The Current Quarter Model and its Forecast Accuracy," *Ritsumeikan Economics*, 56(2), pp. 25–42 (in Japanese).

Inada, Y. (2009) "High Frequency Forecasting Model and Its Application to the Japanese Economy," in L. R. Klein. (ed.) *The Making of National Economic Forecasts*, Edward Elgar, pp. 172–197.

Inada, Y. (2011) "Current Quarter Model Forecasts and Consensus Forecasts," in S. Ichimura and L. R. Klein (eds.) *Macroeconometric Modeling of Japan*, pp. 393–409.

Inada, Y. (2014) "Large Drop in Consumption after the Tax Increase," Economic Classroom, Nihon Keizai Shinbunsha, July 22 (in Japanese).

Klein, L. R. and Sojo, E. (1989) "Combinations of High-frequency Data in Model-based Forecasting at the Federal Reserve Board," in L. R. Klein and J. Marquez (eds.) *Economics in Theory and Practice: An Electric Approach*, Dordrecht: Kluwer, pp. 3–16.

Klein, L. R. and Park, J. Y. (1993) "Economic Forecasting at High-frequency Intervals," *Journal of Forecasting*, 12, pp. 301–319.

Klein, L. R. and Park, J. Y. (1995) "The University of Pennsylvania Model for High-Frequency Economic Forecasting," *Economic and Financial Modeling,* Autumn, pp. 95–146.

Ogawa, R. and Inada, Y. (2013) "The Development of Fast and Accurate Preliminary GRP Estimates," APIR Discussion Paper Series No. 33, April (in Japanese).

Chapter 3

Utilization and Precision of the US Current Quarter Model

Yuzo Kumasaka

President and CEO, IT Economy Advisors, LLC, USA

Professor Lawrence R. Klein originally developed the current quarter model (CQM) in the late 1980s as a complement to the traditional quarterly macroeconomic model. Although the traditional quarterly macroeconomic model is useful for policymakers and economists when it comes to putting together economic forecasts and simulation studies for short- and medium-term (1–3 years), it is not adequate for grasping current economic conditions. Understanding what is happening *now* in the economy is very important not only for policymakers and economists but also for investors and business managers at any time. For example, they all want to know what the economy is doing in the current quarter — how quickly the economy is recovering, how fast it is slowing down, and when it is bottoming out.

For example, advance real GDP growth rate for 2013Q4 was announced to be 3.2%. However, it is not true that the economy was growing at an annual rate of 3.2% every day for that quarter. It is more realistic to understand that the economy repeatedly moved up and down, and created an upward or downward trend (Figure 1).

It is important for economic policymakers (monetary policymakers in particular) as well as investors and company managers to grasp the speed of the current economy (the economic growth rate), the strength of its trend and a turning point for the economy as quickly as possible. However, that is extremely difficult as the Fed economists judge the current economy by saying, as they often do in FOMC statement, "economic activity is expanding at a 'moderate' (or modest) pace". CQM was constructed to fill this knowledge gap.

CQM focuses on economic forecasts for the current and next quarters only. CQM comprises the statistical relationships between about 90 monthly economic and financial indicators, and the main entries in the quarterly national income product accounts (NIPA). The CQM is a purely econometric system with no personal data adjustment. Therefore, CQM is often referred to as a "Go by the Numbers" forecast. Whenever high-frequency indicators are available, partial information about the economy can be updated, revising the current and next quarter forecasts. Since there is no personal adjustment in the CQM, on a forward rolling basis, CQM forecasts are able to identify continuous changes in the economy. We can therefore repeat CQM forecasts of the main entries in NIPA every week and discern trends in the economy or the turning points.

1. How to Make a CQM Forecast

We can explain how CQM works by the performance of forecasting real GDP for 2013Q4. CQM uses about 90 monthly economic indicators (Table 1) and estimates 11 components in the personal consumption expenditure sector, 10 components in the fixed investment sector, 7 components in the inventories sector, 7 components in the international trade sector and 11 components in the government sector on the expenditure side of NIPA. Each component on the expenditure side consists of nominal and real figures, and a price deflator. CQM also estimates 39 nominal components on the income side of NIPA. CQM estimates bridge equations between the monthly economic indicators and NIPA components because the monthly economic indicators are basic statistics composing the NIPA components.

Table 1. Main monthly indicators released in January 2014

Date	Monthly indicators	Date	Monthly indicators
2	Construction spending (2)	15	Producer price indexes (1)
3	Automobile sales (1)		Consumer price indexes (1)
6	Factory orders (2)	17	Housing starts (1)
7	International trade (2)		Industrial production index (1)
8	Consumer credit (2)	28	Durable goods orders (Advance) (1)
9	Employment (1)	30	GDP (2013Q4, Advance)
13	Treasury budget (1)	31	Personal income/consumption expenditure (1)
14	Import/export prices (1)		
	Retail sales (1)		Agricultural prices (0)
	Business inventories (2)		

Number in () indicates the months lagged for the release of each actual monthly economic indicator.

Just as employment statistics such as employment, average hourly earnings and average workweek in each industry are usually released on the first Friday of each month, so are most of the other monthly economic indicators also announced on a similar schedule every month. For example, the releases of main economic indicators in January 2014 are illustrated in Table 1. Most of the monthly economic indicators in Table 1 are the figures of the previous month (i.e. December), but construction spending, factory order (shipments of manufactured goods), the trade balance, business inventories, and consumer credit have a 2-month lag (i.e. November). Only agricultural prices reflect the figures for the current month (i.e. January).

CQM makes statistical bridge equations between monthly economic indicators and their corresponding components in NIPA. Whenever new monthly economic indicators are released, CQM estimates their bridge equations and forecasts their corresponding NIPA components. For example, retail sale statistics are released in the middle of every month. CQM estimates the bridge equation between each category in retail sales and its corresponding component of the nominal consumer spending (PCE) in NIPA. For example, when November retail sales of automobiles and parts dealers are released in the middle of December in 2013, CQM estimates the bridge equation between retail sales of automobiles and parts dealers and nominal PCE of automobiles for the sample period of 1960m1-(January) — 2013m11(November). In addition, CQM forecasts using ARIMA, retail sales of automobiles and parts for the period 2013m12 (December) — 2014m3 (March). Therefore, CQM can forecast the nominal PCE of automobiles for the period 2013m12–2014m3. In this case, the actual figures for October and November retail sales of automobiles and parts dealers were used to forecast the nominal PCE of automobiles for 2013Q4 (m10–m12). When December retail sales are released January in 2014, CQM can forecast the nominal PCE of automobiles for 2013Q4 from the bridge equation which uses all the actual figures for retail sales of automobiles and parts dealers for 2013m10–2013m12. Likewise, CQM applies total retail sales to the bridge equations for proprietors' income and corporate profits on the income side of NIPA.

Figure 1 illustrates the changes of real GDP forecasts calculated on both the expenditure and income sides by CQM when economic indicators were released every week for the period of 9 August 2013–17 January 2014. GDP is aggregated by its NIPA components forecasted by CQM.

Figure 1 shows the changes in the growth rates of the real GDPs that CQM forecasted every week from the week of 9 August 2013 to the week of 17 January 2014. The triangular symbol ▲ and square symbol ▪ show the real GDPs on the expenditure and income sides respectively which were forecasted every week by CQM. The circular symbol • gives the average of the forecasts of the real GDPs on both the expenditure and income sides. Although economic theory tells us that GDPs on the expenditure, income and production sides must be equal to one, they are different in practice because the basic data series that compose NIPA statistics are not perfect. That is why the Bureau of Economic Analysis (BEA) creates a statistical discrepancy (SD) on the income side and

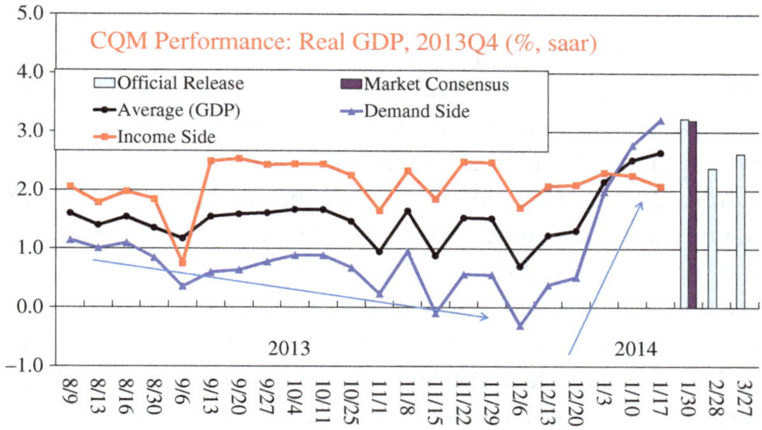

Figure 1. Real GDP forecasts on both the expenditure and income sides for 2014Q3 by CQM (%, saar)

calculates the SD to make the GDP on the income side equal to the GDP on the expenditure side. This does not necessarily mean that GDP calculated from the expenditure side is more correct than GDP calculated on the income side. It is reasonable to assume that true GDP is somewhere between the two. Since SD is not a random data series but a serially correlated time series data, CQM forecasts SD using ARIMA. Therefore, CQM produces GDPs on both the expenditure and income sides independently.

It is one of the characteristics of CQM forecasts to always judge the economy from both the expenditure and income sides. The more actual figures of monthly economic indicators are used in the current quarter CQM updates, the closer GDP forecasts on both the expenditure and income sides tend to be. This is seen in most cases for CQM forecasts, which is reasonable based on the economic theory.

We can show in detail how we could judge the current economic conditions based on Figure 1:

- Employment statistics are usually updated at the beginning of the month. CQM forecasts updated employment statistics as follows: July employment in the August 9 CQM forecast, August employment in the September 6 CQM forecast, September employment in the October 25 CQM forecast, October employment in the November 8 CQM forecast, November employment in the December 6 CQM forecast, December employment in the January 10 CQM forecast. The release of the September employment statistics was delayed until October 25 due to the federal government shutdown. Actual figures of monthly economic indicators for 2013Q4 (October–December) began to be updated by CQM forecasts after November 8.

- The actual figures for construction spending, international trade, business inventories, shipments of manufactured goods and consumer credit were updated in the December CQM forecasts because these monthly economic indicators have a 2-month lag before the actual figures are released.
- In the CQM forecasts from August 9 to December 6, the growth rate of real GDP on the expenditure side was forecasted very low, in the range 0–1.0% with a slightly downward trend. This is because monthly economic indicators released during the period August 9–December 6 in 2013 that affect components of the NIPA expenditure side gradually deteriorated. The Fed postponed reducing its asset purchases of $85 billion per month at the September 18 FOMC meeting because the economy was not recovering as the Fed had expected. Indeed, CQM forecasts of 2013Q4 GDP in Figure 1 show explicitly the economic slowdown until December 6.
- On the other hand, the growth rate of real GDP on the income side was forecasted to be 2–2.5% for 2013Q4 during the period September 13–January 17 because monthly economic indicators that affect components of the NIPA income side released during the period September 13–January 17 did not show the economic slowdown.
- In this way, if the economy is slowing down on the expenditure side without any sign of the economic slowdown on the income side, we can judge that the economic slowdown seen from the expenditure side will be temporary or not be so serious.
- CQM forecasts after December 13 started to use more actual figures of monthly economic indicators for 2013Q4 such as construction spending, international trade, business inventories, shipments of manufactured goods and consumer credit. As CQM updated more

actual figures of the monthly economic indicators for 2013Q4, real GDP on the expenditure side was revised upward sharply. The CQM forecast on January 17 showed the growth rate of real GDP on the expenditure side to be 3.2%, which was equal to the Advance GDP released on January 30.

- On the other hand, there were no significant revisions in the growth rates of real GDP on the income side, which was in a range of 2–2.5%. This suggests that Preliminary or Final 2013Q4 GDP will be lower than the Advance GDP. This is because true economic growth rate is reasonably assumed to be somewhere between the real GDPs on both the expenditure and income sides. More of the basic data that compose NIPA components are available in the Preliminary and Final GDP figures than for the Advance GDP. BEA released the Preliminary real GDP figure of 2.4% on February 28 and the Final GDP figure of 2.6% on March 27, which was close to the average growth rate of real GDPs on both the expenditure and income sides on January 17.

2. CQM Forecast Performance for the Worst Period of 2008Q4 After Lehman Shock

It was in 2008Q4 that the worst effects of the Lehman shock were felt by the US economy. We can better understand the characteristics of CQM forecast by looking at the CQM forecast performance for 2008Q4.

Figure 2 shows the CQM forecasts every week from August 8 in 2008 to January 23 in 2009. As seen in Figure 2, the growth rate of real GDP on the expenditure side declined to about –2% in the August 15 CQM forecast and it was revised downward sharply after the September CQM forecasts, reaching –10% in the November 14 CQM forecast. Also, real GDP on the income side began to show a negative growth rate in September and followed quickly the sharp economic slowdown on the expenditure side. In the event, the growth rate of real GDP on the income side reached –7% in the November 14 CQM forecast. We see that CQM was able to show how serious the current economic slowdown in 2008Q4 was. After late November CQM forecasts, CQM started to revise upward real GDPs on both the expenditure and income sides. In the January 23 CQM forecast before the release of Advance 2008Q4 GDP, the growth

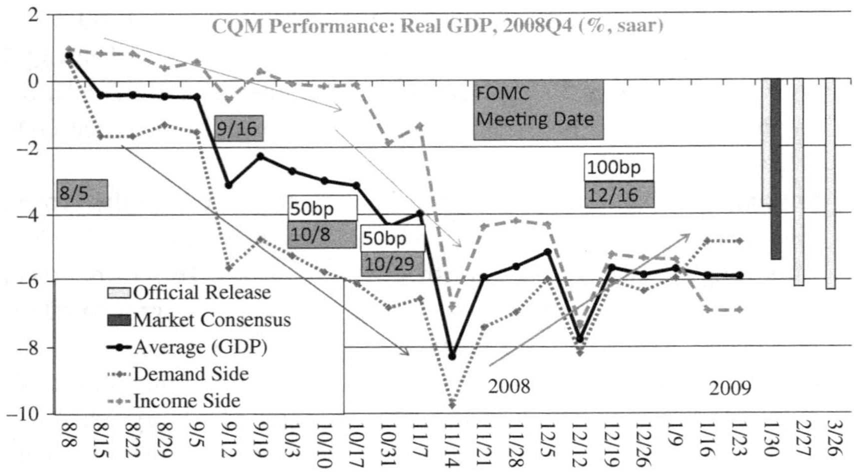

Figure 2. CQM forecast performance of real GDP for 2008Q4 (%, saar)

rates of real GDP were forecasted to be –4.9% on the expenditure side and –6.9% on the income side. The average growth rate of real GDPs on both sides was –5.9%. As the bar graphs display in Figure 2, the Advance real GDP growth rate was –3.8%, but it was revised downward to –6.2% in the Preliminary real GDP and to –6.3% in the Final real GDP, very close to the average growth rate of real GDPs calculated from CQM forecast. Based on the July 2013 comprehensive revision of NIPA, the economic growth rate for 2008Q4 became –8.9%, which justifies the severe CQM forecast on November 14. By observing the CQM forecasts for 2008Q4, one could expect substantial monetary easing would be undertaken in September–November 2008.

The Fed had five FOMC meetings during the period of CQM forecasting 2008Q4 GDP (Figure 2), and at the first of these, gave the following economic outlook:

- FOMC statement on August 5, 2013

"Over time, the substantial easing of monetary policy, combined with ongoing measures to foster market liquidity, should help to promote moderate economic growth. ... Inflation has been high, spurred by the earlier increases

in the prices of energy and some other commodities, and some indicators of inflation expectations have been elevated".

As of August 5, the Fed remained optimistic for promoting moderate economic growth, but was concerned about inflation.

- FOMC statement on September 16, 2013

"*Economic growth appears to have slowed recently, partly reflecting a softening of household spending. ... Over time, the substantial easing of monetary policy, combined with ongoing measures to foster market liquidity, should help to promote moderate economic growth*".

As of September 16, although the Fed recognized the recent economic slowdown, they were still optimistic for the economy with moderate growth. CQM indicated that the growth rate of real GDP on the expenditure side was declining significantly to about –6%.

- FOMC statement on October 8, 2013

"*Incoming economic data suggest that the pace of economic activity has slowed markedly in recent months. .... The Federal Open Market Committee has decided to lower its target for the federal funds rate 50 basis points to 1-1/2 percent. The Committee took this action in light of evidence pointing to a weakening of economic activity and a reduction in inflationary pressures*".

As of October 8, the Fed admitted that the economy had recently slowed down. For this reason, the Fed cut the federal funds rate 50 basis points to 1.5%. Even so, it would have been unlikely for the Fed to recognize that the economy would be plunging to –10% growth rate. Rather the Fed joined the Bank of Canada, the Bank of England, the European Central Bank, the Federal Reserve, Sveriges Riksbank and the Swiss National Bank in a policy of reducing interest rates.

- FOMC statement on October 29, 2013

"*The pace of economic activity appears to have slowed markedly, owing importantly to a decline in consumer expenditures*".

"*The Federal Open Market Committee decided today to lower its target for the federal funds rate 50 basis points to 1 percent*".

As of October 29, the Fed recognized the sharp economic slowdown as being due mainly to weakening consumer spending. However, the CQM forecast on October 31 showed that the economic slowdown was due to deterioration in net exports. The CQM forecast on November 14 suggested that the economy had plunged further because not only net exports but also personal consumption expenditure had deteriorated. The CQM forecasted on November 14 that the growth rate of real personal consumption expenditure would be –5.5% for 2008Q4.

- FOMC statement on December 16, 2013

  "*Overall, the outlook for economic activity has weakened further. ... The Federal Open Market Committee decided today to establish a target range for the federal funds rate of 0 to 1/4 percent*".

As of December 16, the Fed cut federal funds rate by 100 basis points to 0–0.5% because they thought that the economy had weakened further. Indeed, the CQM shows large negative growth rates of real GDPs on both the expenditure and income sides, but it suggested that the economy had bottomed out since November 14 (Figure 2). Namely, the Fed missed that the economy was bottoming out. It is reasonable to think that the Fed should have cut federal funds rate by 100 basis points at the FOMC meeting on September 16 or October 8.

Comparing CQM forecasts with FOMC statements, CQM has the following advantages:

1. CQM can always determine the current economic situation from the numbers and trends by making CQM forecasts weekly on a forward rolling basis.
2. CQM is able to reveal the turning points of the economy at least 1 month earlier than the Fed economists (and the market) recognize.
3. Since CQM is a purely econometric system with no personal data adjustment, we can judge the current economic condition objectively. There is no bias for or against certain monthly economic indicators because CQM is referred to as a "Go by the Numbers" forecast.
4. CQM always considers the economy from both the expenditure and income (or production) sides.

3. CQM is Better than Forward Guidance for Fed's Monetary Policy

Fed economists always say that "Monetary policy is (incoming) data dependent" and that "Monetary policy depends on how the economy is evolving". No Fed economists disagree that monetary policy should depend on the current economic conditions.

They judge, however, the current economic conditions in most FOMC statements by saying that "economic activity has been expanding at a moderate pace". They have never shown the current economic condition by figures and trends. Therefore, they have introduced Forward Guidance on which monetary policy depends.

Table 2 shows how the Fed economists have changed their forward guidance. Federal Reserve Bank of Dallas President Richard W. Fisher classified forward guidance into two types: "Odysseus" or "Apollo" (Fisher, 2014).

The changes in forward guidance show the fact that the Fed could not start increasing interest rates by forward guidance. Nonetheless, the Fed added the sentence "the Committee judges that it can be patient in beginning to normalize the stance of monetary policy" in the FOMC at December 17 in 2014. At a news conference after the FOMC meeting, Fed Chair Janet Yellen told that "patient" meant the policy-setting Federal Open Market Committee was unlikely to hike rates for "at least a couple of meetings", meaning April of next year at the earliest. Namely, monetary policy is dependent on calendar, instead of incoming data.

Although the US economy grew at 4.6 and 5.0% respectively for 2014Q2 and Q3, the Fed did not increase interest rates in 2014Q4 because monetary policy actually depended on forward guidance. If monetary policy were incoming data dependent like CQM forecasts, the Fed could increase interest rates immediately. As of January 2, 2015 there were only two Fed economists who recommended raising interest rates immediately. Philadelphia Fed President Charles Plosser said "A forecasting tool developed by the Federal Reserve recommends that US interest rates should be hiked immediately to keep pace with the improving economy (Dotsey *et al.*, 2014)". Cleveland Fed President Loretta Mester said on the Fox Business Network television channel on January 2 "I do believe that

Table 2. Changes in forward guidance (FG) shown in FOMC statements

Date of FOMC statements	Forward Guidance (FG)	Classification by Richard Fisher
28 Jan. 2009	FFR = 0–0.25%: **For some time**	
18 Mar. 2009	FFR = 0–0.25%: **For an extended period**	
9 Aug. 2011	FFR = 0–0.25%: **at least through mid-2013**	Odysseus Type (Calendar-base FG)
25 Jan. 2012	FFR = 0–0.25%: **at least through late 2014**	
13 Sep.2012	FFR = 0–0.25%: **at least through mid-2013**	
12 Dec. 2012	**Unemployment Rate = 6.5%** (as threshold) A highly accommodative stance of monetary policy will remain appropriate "**Considerable time**" after QE3 ends and the economic recovery strengthens	Apollo Type (FG dependent on the Oracle of Apollo at Delphi)
30 Jul. 2014	From the threshold of 6.5% unemployment rate to a **labor market condition index**. **Keep FFR below levels as normal in the longer run**, even after employment rate and inflation are near mandate-consistent level.	
17 Dec. 2014	The Committee judges that it can be "**patient**" in beginning to normalize the stance of monetary policy. It likely will be appropriate to maintain the 0 to 1/4 percent target range for the federal funds rate **for a considerable time** following the end of its asset purchase program in October.	
27 Jan. 2015	Dropped "**a considerable time**"	

FFR: Target of Federal Funds Rate.

inflation will gradually move back to our target, so I could imagine interest rates going up in the first half of the year".

The 23 January 2015 CQM forecasts, relying on incoming data, can tell that the Fed should raise interest rates immediately. Figures 3–6 show the CQM forecasts of real GDPs and real aggregated indexes for 2014Q4 and 2015Q1 until January 23 in 2015.

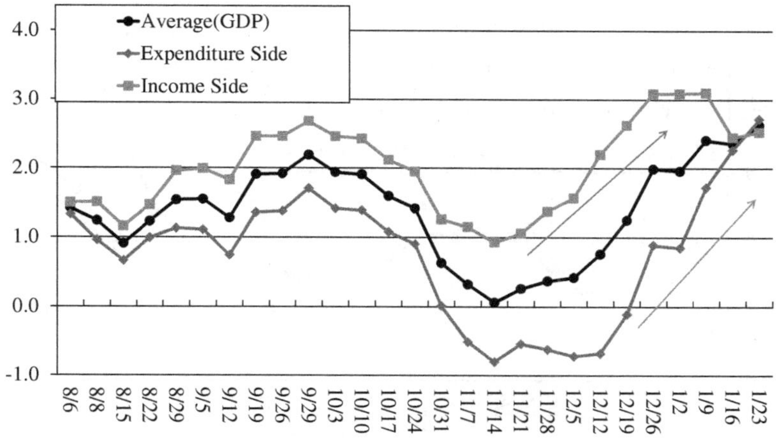

Figure 3. CQM forecast of real GDPs for 2014Q4, (%, saar)

Figure 3 shows that real GDP on the expenditure side has been sharply improving since the December 19 CQM forecast as had been expected by the upward trend in real GDP on the income side since the November 21 CQM forecast. The January 23 CQM forecasts the growth rate of real GDP on the expenditure side to be 2.72% for 2014Q4 and that on the income side to be 2.53% (Figure 3). The average growth rate of real GDPs on both the sides reached 2.63% (Figure 3). CQM forecasts of real aggregated indexes also illustrate the steady economic expansion since late October or mid-November (Figure 4). As of January 23, the growth rates of real aggregated indexes are forecasted to be in a range of 3.3–4.2% for 2014Q4. These growth rates of real GDPs and real aggregated indexes as well as their upward trends suggest that there is no need for the Fed to keep its zero interest rate policy.

As seen in Figures 5 and 6, not only CQM forecasts for 2014Q4 but also those for 2015Q1 suggest that the Fed should start to normalize its monetary policy.

The Fed has two main targets of maximizing employment and price stability. The minutes of the 16–17 December 2014 FOMC meeting released on 7 January 2015 say the following:

- *Most participants agreed that it would be useful to state that the Committee judges that it can be patient in beginning to normalize the*

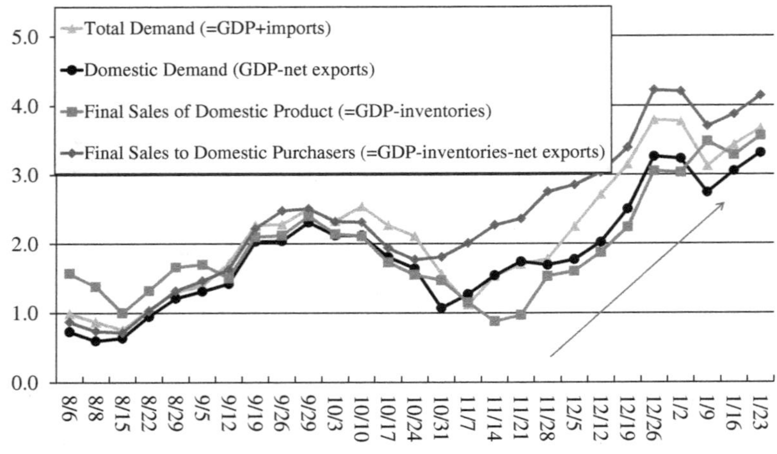

Figure 4. CQM forecast of real aggregated indexes for 2014Q4, (%, saar)

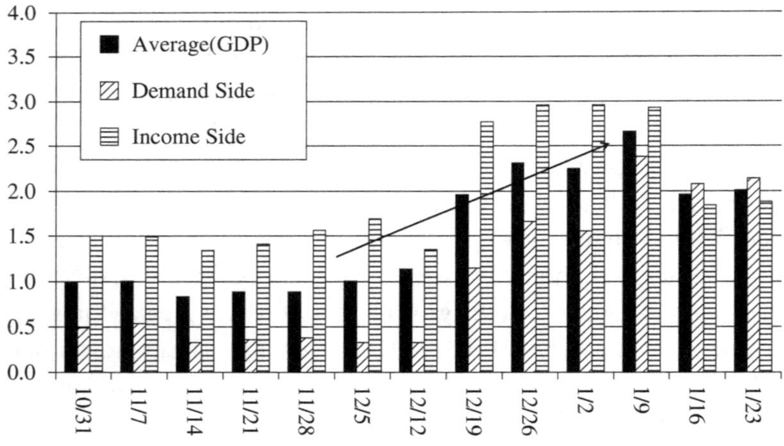

Figure 5. CQM forecast of real GDPs for 2015Q1, (%, saar)

stance of monetary policy; they noted that such language would provide more flexibility to adjust policy in response to incoming information than the previous language, which had tied the beginning of normalization to the end of the asset purchase program.

- *With lower energy prices and the stronger dollar likely to keep inflation below target for some time, it was noted that the Committee*

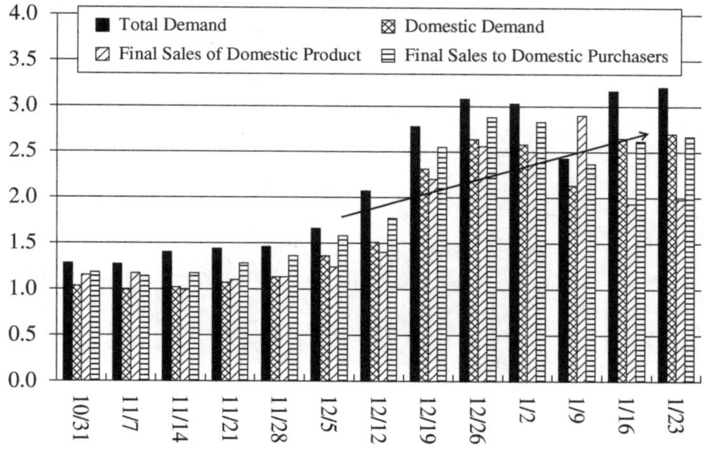

Figure 6. CQM forecast of real aggregated indexes for 2015Q1, (%, saar)

might begin normalization at a time when core inflation was near current levels, although in that circumstance participants would want to be reasonably confident that inflation will move back toward 2% over time.

Since CQM forecasts the current economy by using incoming information (economic indicators), CQM can conclude that the real economy has been steadily expanding for 2014Q4 and will grow steadily for 2015Q1, which leads to the conclusion that the Fed should normalize its monetary policy. Since the US economy grew at annual rate of 4.6 and 5% respectively for 2014Q2 and Q3, the Fed economists must recognize the recent steady economic expansion. Indeed, the economy has been growing much faster than the "moderate growth" Fed economists had forecasted.

The main reason why the Fed does not start to raise interest rates seems to be that the current inflation rate is "well below" the Fed's target of 2%. Indeed, the growth rate of headline inflation from a year ago has not exceeded 2% since 2012Q2. The January 23 CQM forecast suggests the growth rate of headline inflation to be 1.1 and 0.6% for 2014Q4 and 2015Q1, respectively (Figure 7). Although Plosser and Dallas Fed

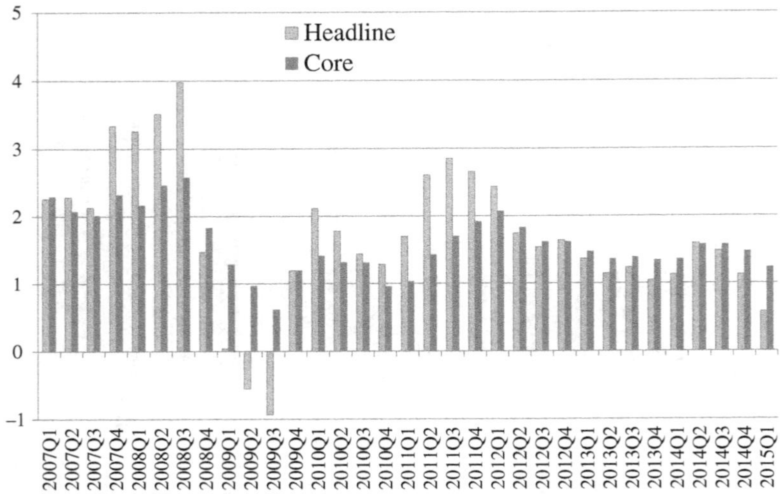

Figure 7. CQM forecasts of headline inflation and core inflation for 2014Q4 and 2015Q1 (% from a year ago, saar)

President Richard Fisher, who have been skeptics of Fed's easy-money policies, often expressed concern that the Fed might wait too long to raise rates, dove Fed economists including Minneapolis Fed President Narayana Kocherlakota and Chicago Fed President Charles Evans, who are the strongest supporters of aggressive efforts to spur growth, worried that the central bank was preparing to increase rates too soon. Evans was reported as saying on January 7 that he was very concerned that, by his forecast, inflation won't return to Fed's 2% goals in 2018, even if the Fed does not begin to raise rates until next year. But he also suggested that he would be open to raising rates this year, should data come in stronger than expected, or if the rates rises are shallow enough, they would not keep inflation from returning to more healthy levels (Reuters, 2015, January 7)."

"Price Stability", one of Fed's targets, has come to mean achieving a 2% inflation rate, though the monetary policy used to prevent inflation or deflation from accelerating from a certain range of 0–2%. In the real world, there is no creeping inflation that will gradually increase from 1 to 2% for the next 2 years. Once inflation starts increasing, it will instantly exceed Fed's 2% target by far. Also, if the Fed keeps a zero interest rate policy too long, its cost will exceed its' benefits. For example, Table 3

Table 3. Personal interest income and payment ($Billion, saar)

	2008	2009	2010	2011	2012	2013
Income	1362	1264	1195	1232	1256	1255
Payments	290	274	251	241	242	247
Net	1072	990	944	990	1014	1008
2008 — Year income		97	167	130	106	106
2008 — Year payments		16	39	48	48	43
2008 — Year net		82	128	82	58	64

displays how seriously zero interest rate policy has been affecting personal interest income more than personal interest payments. Since nominal residential investment was about $570 billion in 2014, it is understood that the negative effect of zero interest rate policy on household is very serious.

4. Accuracy of CQM Forecast

It is advance GDP figures that markets pay attention most. In order to calculate preliminary GDP, the BEA must assume the figures of the last month in the quarter for each of the trade balance (the import and export), business inventories, construction spending and shipments of manufactured goods. On the other hand, CQM forecasts these figures by using ARIMA. If BEA's assumptions of the figures are close to CQM's forecasts, the advance GDP tends to be close to CQM's forecast of the GDP.

We can check CQM performance by comparing CQM forecasts of real GDP with BEA's Advance GDP for 53 quarters during the period of 2000Q4–2013Q4. Since we compare the CQM forecasts of GDP with advance GDP, the GDP forecasts on the expenditure side are used more adequately than the average GDP forecasts on both the expenditure and income sides.

Figure 8 illustrates the last CQM forecasts of real GDP on the expenditure side for each quarter with Advance real GDP in terms of annual growth rate from the previous quarter. That is to say, if the CQM forecast is equal to the Advance real GDP, then the plot is on the line of

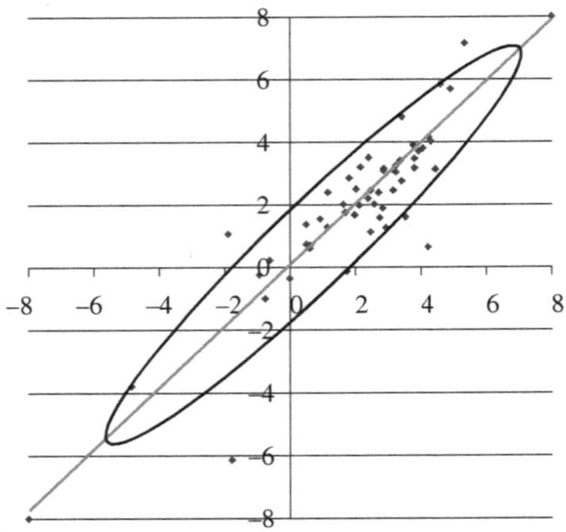

Fgiure 8. Last CQM forecasts of real GDP before the release of advance GDP (X axis) vs. advance real GDP (Y axis) (%, saar)

45 degree from the origin. If CQM overestimates (underestimates) advance real GDP, then the plot locates to the right (left) area of the 45 degree line.

In the last CQM forecasts, actual figures for 3 months in the forecasting quarter were updated for most of the monthly economic indicators while actual figures for only 2 months were updated for international trade, business inventories, shipments of manufactured goods, construction spending and consumer credit. As seen in Figure 8, the plots were scattered very close to the 45 degree line, suggesting that CQM forecasts were quite accurate.

In order to understand the accuracy of CQM forecasts statistically, we can make a regression analysis of the Advance real GDP on the last CQM forecasts of GDP as follows:

Y: Advance real GDP (%, saar)

X: Last CQM forecast of real GDP on the expenditure side (%, saar)

$$Y = 0.939801 * X \tag{1}$$

(t-value = 16.9)

Sample period: 2000Q4–2013Q4, R2_ (Adjusted R-square value): 0.69, D-W: 2.05.

Equation 1 without constant term shows 0.69 for the adjusted R-squared, which is quite good relationship for *Y* and *X* variables in terms of growth rates. That the last CQM forecast of real GDP is close to the Advance real GDP is a necessary condition for understanding that weekly CQM forecasts up to the last forecast are right to represent the economic conditions.

Figure 9 compares the Advance real GDP with CQM forecast of real GDP on the expenditure side about 1 month before the release of the Advance GDP. Then, the only economic monthly indicators in the CQM forecast that have actual figures for all 3 months of the forecasting quarter are employment statistics and agricultural prices. Plots in Figure 9 spread wider than those in Figure 8. This is because most of the economic indicators in the CQM forecast have actual figures for only 2 months of the forecasting quarter. Construction spending, international trade, business inventories, shipments of manufactured goods and consumer credit have actual figures for only 1 month.

Figure 10 compares the CQM forecast of real GDP about 2 months before the release of the Advance real GDP with the Advance real GDP. In the CQM forecasts, only employment statistics and agricultural prices have actual figures for 2 months of the forecasting quarter. Most of the

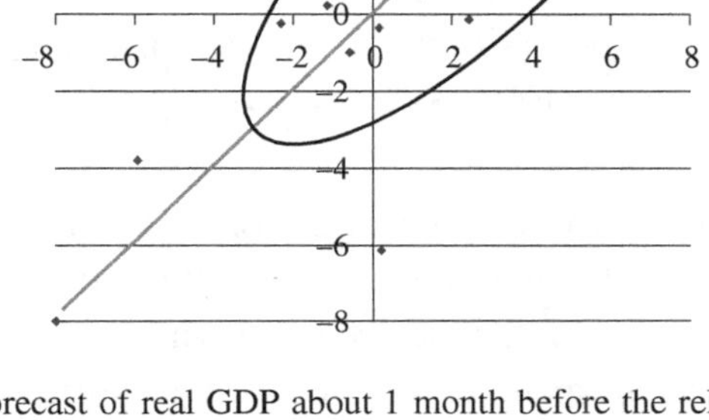

Figure 9. CQM forecast of real GDP about 1 month before the release of advance real GDP (*X* axis) vs. advance real GDP (*Y* axis) (%, saar)

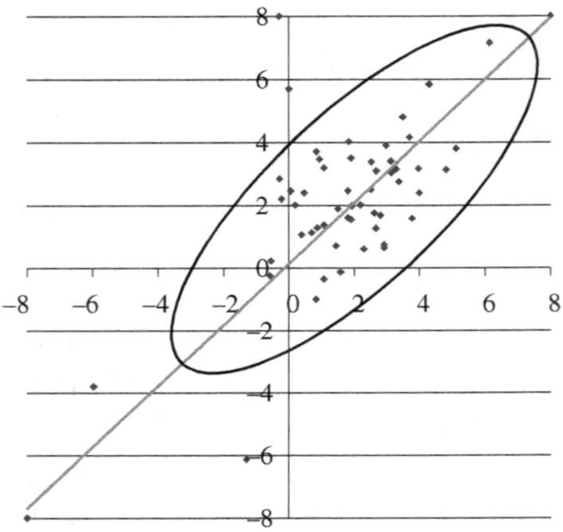

Figure 10. CQM forecast of real GDP about 2 months before the release of advance real GDP (*X* axis) vs. advance real GDP (*Y* axis) (%, saar)

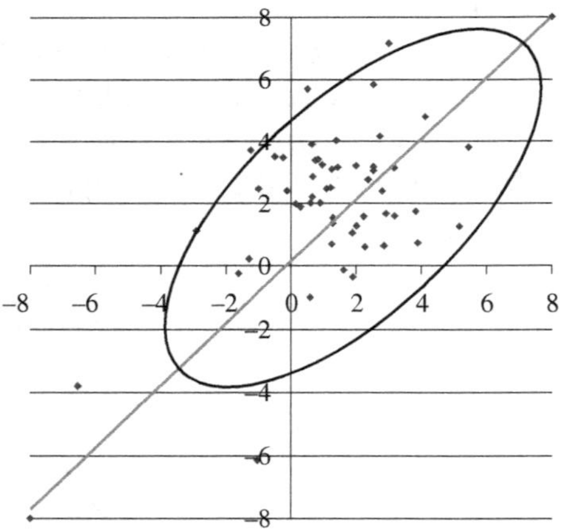

Figure 11. CQM forecast of real GDP about 3 months before the release of advance real GDP (*X* axis) vs. advance real GDP (*Y* axis) (%, saar)

economic indicators have actual figures for only 1 month. There are no actual figures for construction spending, international trade, business inventories, shipments of manufactured goods and consumer credit. There is no obvious improvement in the forecast performance in Figure 9, compared with Figure 10.

Figure 11 compares the CQM forecast of real GDP about 3 months before the release of the Advance real GDP with the Advance real GDP. This shows the CQM performance when only employment statistics and agricultural prices have actual figures for 1 month of the forecasting quarter. Other monthly economic indicators used in the CQM forecast have no actual figures for the forecasting quarter. Plots in Figure 11 spread much wider than those in Figures 9 and 10. In other words, CQM increases its forecast performance sharply once it begins to update actual figures of monthly economic indicators for the forecasting quarter.

5. Conclusions

CQM is the best tool to grasp the current economic conditions because CQM produces purely data-dependent forecasts and shows how the economy is evolving by figures and trends. Many economists often focus on the expenditure sides of NIPA only such as personal consumption expenditure, fixed investment, inventories, exports and imports, and government consumption expenditures/gross investment in order to judge the current economic conditions, whereas CQM always looks at both the expenditure and income sides.

There are ongoing debates about how monetary policy can be determined. For example, Plosser recommends a systemic approach to monetary policy, where policy rules such as Taylor rules benchmark the stance of monetary policy. On the other hand, Kocherlakota insists that the Fed is better off using its own best judgment rather than relying on a policy rule when it comes to deciding rate policy. CQM lies between the policy rules' approach and the judgment approach. CQM always proposes the current economic conditions by figures and trends, leaving it to economists themselves to decide the monetary policy with their judgment.

CQM will play an increasingly important role for policymakers and investors to make quick and accurate decisions because handling frequency data becomes much easier as the IT revolution continues to progress. When Prof. Lawrence R. Klein created Project LINK consisting of quarterly macroeconomic models in the world, he planned to make a CQM LINK system for the world. If we could make such a CQM LINK system, we could grasp the current economic conditions in the world instantly through CQM forecast in each country as soon as economic information in any country was released. This would make a significant contribution to economic policymakers in the world.

References

Dotsey, M., Charles, I. P. and Keith, S. (2014) Special Report "Monetary Policy Report: Using Rules for Benchmarking," Federal Reserve Bank of Philadelphia, December.

Fisher, W. R. (2014) "Forward Guidance," Federal Reserve Bank of Dallas, April 4.

Reuters (2015) "HIGHLIGHTS-Recent remarks by U.S. Federal Reserve officials," January 7.

Chapter 4

Using the High-Frequency Forecast Method to Estimate Local Government GRP

Ryoh Ogawa

Osaka City University

1. Introduction

Local governments must stay informed about local economic conditions in order to make and carry out policies, which contribute to the development and stability of the region. To draft these policies properly, it is always necessary to check the latest values of various economic indicators.

Local government gross regional product (GRP) is the most comprehensive indicator of local economic conditions, but local governments' statistical authorities often take a long time to release their final estimate of the GRP. In the case of Japan, each prefecture publishes its final estimate of GRP almost 2 years after the final estimate of national GDP is released. This means that Japanese local governments have had to manage their policies without important information on recent economic conditions.

One of the reasons why this delay occurs is because government statistical authorities need to collect many kinds of relevant statistics to make these estimates, which takes a considerable amount of time. Additionally, the national government takes a long time to systematically process statistical data into regional units. The national statistical authority's strict regulations contribute to the delayed release of GRP estimates in Japan, and they must be reformed to increase the speed of GRP releases.

As an alternative approach, some Japanese prefectures are using the limited amount of data at their disposal to make quick estimates of their own GRP. However, these quick estimates often differ from the official final estimates that are released later, and therefore many prefectures do not make quick estimates of their own GRP.[1]

This chapter presents a new method of making quick estimates of GRP that is superior in terms of both release speed and accuracy. In the past, quick estimates of GRP were calculated by adding together the private and public expenditures and industrial sectors of output that are individually estimated using regression analysis. While this method was useful for analyzing the movement of specific elements of GRP (e.g. consumption, investment), any errors in those individual elements' statistics would affect the accuracy of the overall estimate. In contrast, in the new approach presented here, GRP itself is regressed on a limited number of statistics through principal component analysis. This method is based on one of the high-frequency forecast methods developed by Professor Lawrence Klein of Pennsylvania University in the late 1980s and has been used to make forecasts of the US and Japanese economy as a part of the Current Quarter Model since the 1990s (Klein and Sojo, 1989; Klein and Park, 1993,1995; Inada, 2010). The method involves selecting monthly statistics that both represent business conditions well and are released promptly, using principal component analysis to extract fundamental components of regional economy, and then directly estimating the relationship between these components and total GRP.

As such, this method produces estimates of GRP levels for the recent past and can also be used to make short-term forecasts of future GRP movements. Inada (2010) used this method to make forecasts of Japan's GDP,[2]

[1]According to the Japanese Government's Economic and Social Research Institute, as of April 2008, only 10 local governments were releasing quarterly estimates of their prefecture's GRP.

[2]Inada also uses the method to make short-term forecasts of Japan's GDP at the Asia Pacific Institute of Research (APIR), releasing forecasts on a weekly basis.

showing how this method can be used in conjunction with the principal component analysis model to forecast quarterly GDP. He also demonstrated that this method was more accurate than ESP forecast surveys.[3]

This chapter uses, the same principal component analysis model to make quick estimates of the GRPs of Japanese prefectures. However, because Japanese GRP data are low-frequency (i.e. annual data), making accurate estimations is a challenge. To counter this problem, this study determine its model based on the Akaike information criterion (AIC). This method allows us to choose principal components that efficiently explain each area's business conditions (movement of GRP).

Specifically, this chapter uses this method to forecast GRPs for the six prefectures of the Kansai region: Osaka, Hyogo, Kyoto, Shiga, Nara, and Wakayama. It shows that the quick estimation method presented herein performs well both in terms of the fit of its regression models (which will be tested using interpolation) and its forecast potential (which will be verified using extrapolation).

The rest of the chapter is arranged as follows. Section 2 introduces the GRP estimation method and, through example applications of the method to the six Kansai prefectures' GRPs, it confirms the fit of the method's data. Next, Section 3 tests the accuracy of this method's forecasts. Finally, Section 4 concludes the study and present potential topics for future studies.

2. A New Approach to Making Quick Estimations of GRP

This section demonstrates how to apply the high-frequency forecast method introduced above to make quick estimations of GRP, showing example applications of the method to six prefectures in the Kansai region of Japan.

---

[3]ESP forecast surveys are surveys of the forecasts of a number of private economists. ESP surveys collect economists' forecasts of various important indexes, including the Japanese stock exchange and the exchange rate of the yen, as well as their appraisal of overall business conditions. Based on this data, ESP forecasts ascertain the consensus on future financial movements and the sustainability of current trends.

2.1. Method

Is it possible to estimate GRP figures for the recent past precisely and rapidly, even before they have been officially calculated by a local government? In Japan, the most recent values of several monthly statistics (data) on regional economy, such as production, consumption, and employment statistics, are released to the public with a lag of only 2 or 3 months. It would be ideal if we could take advantage of the immediacy of these monthly statistics and use them as a set of explanatory variables to forecast unknown and recent past GRPs. However, when these monthly data are strongly correlated with each other, multicollinearity problems occur.

As an alternative approach to avoid the problems, prefectures forecast GRP components, such as private and public expenditures and industrial outputs by regression using one or two statistics related to those individual components as explanatory variables. However, each estimations are inaccurate because of the paucity of available and relevant statistics as explanatory variables.

In the new method presented in this chapter, GRP is regressed to principal components of the monthly statistics, fundamental figures that represent trends of regional economy, using the principal component analysis method. This is done to avoid multicollinearity problems. This method basically follows the high-frequency forecast method used by Klein and Sojo (1989), Klein and Park (1993, 1995), and Inada (2010).

This method mainly has dealt with GDP that is available in quarterly frequencies. For instance, Inada (2010) applied this method to estimate Japan's seasonal GDP. On the other hand, GRP data is provided only at yearly intervals, at least in Japan. This lack of availability of samples makes accurate forecasting difficult. Certainly, one solution would be to collect as many past samples as possible. But this would raise new problems, as we would be forced to jumble together time series data calculated using different approaches (e.g. 08SNA, 93SNA, 68SNA, 53SNA) and suffer from a wide variety of structural changes. In addition, we would not be able to obtain necessary long-term monthly statistics for all underlying components and would have to leave out this important data.

Restricted by a small set of about 20 samples, we will attempt to use Akaike's information criterion (AIC) to carefully select the principal

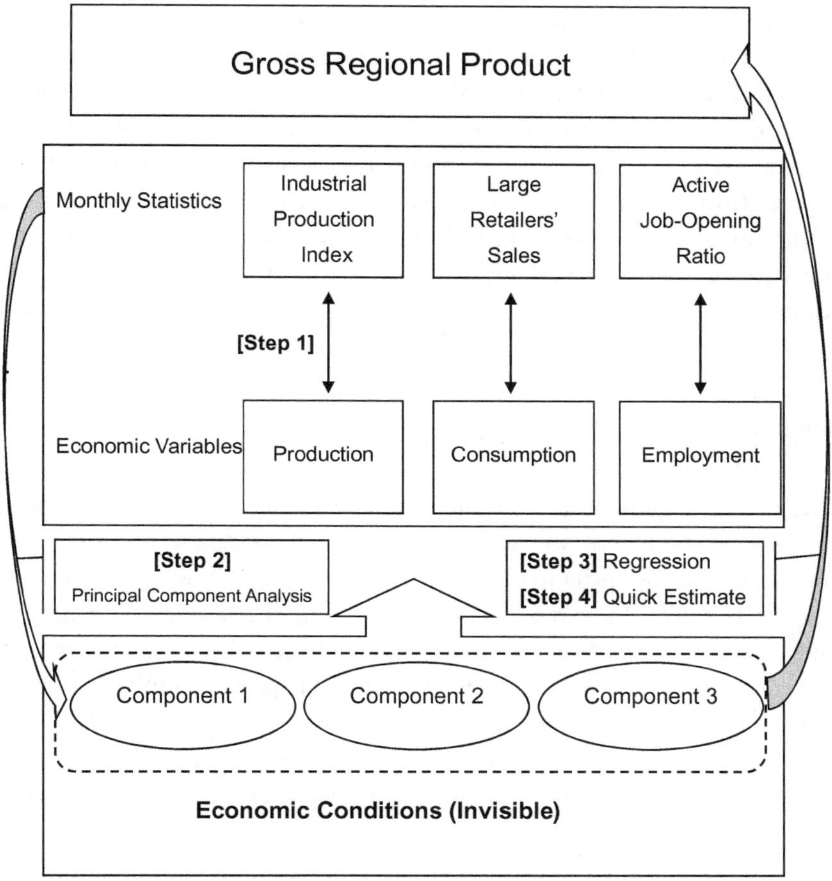

Figure 1. Diagrammatic representation of new quick estimation method

components as the explanatory variables, and test how accurately we can forecast prefectural GRP using this method.

The method consists of the following four steps, explained pictorially in Figure 1.

Step 1: Selecting monthly statistics

In this step, we select monthly statistics that reflect regional economic fluctuations and that are announced to the public promptly. It is important to select a well-balanced set of statistics from each aspect of the economy, such as the consumption, investment, production, and employment. In fact, many Japanese prefectures have already selected monthly statistics in this manner, and are recording the movements of these statistics in diffusion indices (DI) and composite indices (CI) as a means of measuring regional business cycles. When prefectures select these statistical sets, they confirm that each statistic is released quickly and reflects economic conditions well. Therefore, in this chapter, we can reference established statistical sets when constructing local DIs and CIs for quick estimates. Additionally, we find and add original statistics that are closely correlated to GRP if necessary.

Step 2: Extracting the principal components of regional economic fluctuations

After converting monthly data into annual (average) data, we extract the principal components of regional economic fluctuations from these annual data using principal component analysis. Principal component analysis is a well-known analytical method in sociological and psychological fields. In the field of econometrics, principal component analysis is used as a means of selecting variables that prevent multicollinearity from occurring between explanatory variables in regression. Also, this method creates new constructed variables (principal components) with high explanatory potential, thus increasing the accuracy of explanations.

Step 3: Regressing the model equation for forecast and performing interpolation tests

Next, we regress actual values of GRP onto the principal components that are extracted in Step 2 using the ordinary least square method. The number of principal components corresponds to the number of monthly statistics being used. (For example, if we select n number of monthly statistics, we will find the same n number of principal components). If we use all of these as explanatory variables, the accuracy of forecast using an estimation such as ours, with its small sample size, will be undesirable. This is because the low degree of freedom increases the dispersion of forecasted value. Therefore, it is important to narrow down the number of variables used as explanatory variables as much as possible without largely decreasing the goodness of fit. The previous studies have generally chosen principal components in order, starting from those with the largest contribution ratio and stopping when the cumulative contribution ratio of the principal components reaches a peak. In contrast, our method uses the AIC to select the most suitable combination of principal components for the forecast model out of all the possible combinations. This means that we test all the possible combinations of principal components when there is 1 component through to when there is *n* components using the equation $\sum_{i=1}^{n} {}_{n}C_{i}$ and choose the combination that has the smallest AIC value.

Next, we conduct interpolation tests on the selected forecast model to confirm whether or not our choice of monthly variables was appropriate. We calculate the mean absolute percentage error (MAPE) between actual values and estimated levels and growth rates of real GRP, and check the magnitude of the MAPE. This result will demonstrate how well the chosen monthly statistics fit within our forecast model. If the MAPE is relatively high, we have to reconsider the selection of monthly statistics.[4]

Step 4: Making quick estimations of GRP

Using the estimation model, we forecast values of real GRPs for out of samples: The recent past 2 years (periods *t*–1 and *t*–2), the values of which are not yet to have been calculated officially. And then, using the forecasted value that we gain from this process, we calculate the real GRP growth rates. Incidentally, to forecast real GRP levels, we perform the following correction of constant terms:

Fiscal year *t*–2 real GRP (forecast value) =
Fiscal year *t*–2 real growth rate (forecast value) × Fiscal year *t*–3 real GRP (actual value)

Fiscal year *t*–1 real GRP (forecast value) =
Fiscal year *t*–1 real growth rate (forecast value) × Fiscal year *t*–2 real GRP (forecast value)

---

[4]Other monthly statistics should also be considered if the MAPE for the extrapolation tests, to be presented later, is too high.

2.2. Example application of the forecast method on GRP of Kansai prefectures

This section introduces an example application of this forecast method. This is our attempt to forecast (make quick estimations of) GRPs of six prefectures in the Kansai area of Japan (Osaka, Hyogo, Kyoto, Shiga, Nara, and Wakayama) for the 2012 and 2013 fiscal years.

2.2.1. *Selecting monthly statistics (Step 1)*

When selecting monthly statistics, I referred to established sets of monthly coincident indicators used to make local CIs in each prefecture. Osaka, Hyogo, Nara and Wakayama prefectures have made DIs and CIs and have released these to the public. These sets can be used to make quick estimations of the prefectures' real annual GRPs as quickly as the national statistics authority's official GDP announcements. After the new fiscal year begins in April, it takes approximately 2 months for the necessary monthly data of the previous fiscal year to be assembled and announced officially. This means that forecasts for the previous fiscal year become possible in June of the current year. Incidentally, Kyoto and Shiga prefectures have not made their CIs, so to select monthly statistics for these prefectures, I refer to the CIs of other prefectures in Kansai.

When using monthly datasets chosen based on coincident indicator CI series, one may find, after performing the interpolation test in Step 3, that certain prefectures have accuracy problems. In that case, it is necessary to find other monthly statistics that is strongly correlated to the real GRP, and either append it to the existing dataset or replace with it. Following this procedure, I selected the monthly datasets displayed in Table 1. I chose a balanced array of statistics from the employment, consumption, production, and investment. For the Kansai prefectures with relatively small economies (i.e. Kyoto, Shiga, Nara, and Wakayama), we chose to use a national statistical index (the Nikkei Commodity Price Index), which improved the accuracy of our model.[5]

[5]The Nikkei Commodity Price Index is an index that calculates the market value of major commodities, which shift along with even subtle changes in business conditions. It is often used as a model index of business conditions in Japanese economic research.

The time series data for GRP that we used begins in 1996, and so the statistics in Table 1 range from fiscal 1996 to fiscal 2013. Only Shiga prefecture's data differs, ranging from fiscal 1998 to fiscal 2013, because the 1996 and 1997 values of Shiga's shipment index were not available. This index is very closely correlated to Shiga's GRP and without it, the performance of our forecast for Shiga in the interpolation test became much worse.

2.2.2. *Extracting the principal components of regional economic fluctuations (Step 2)*

In this step, we extracted the principal components of economic fluctuations in each prefecture from the statistical data above using principal component analysis. First, we converted monthly data into annual data. Second, after finding the principal components of each region's economy, we named these principal components PC1, PC2, …, PC*n* in order of largest to smallest eigenvalue (contribution rate). The *n* indicates the number of selected statistics. Figure 2 shows each principal component of Osaka Prefecture as an example. This figure demonstrates the general trend for all of Kansai's prefectures, namely, PC1 to PC4 all shifted significantly, while PC5 and over were comparatively stable; the latter principal components would likely have been excluded by the previous studies' selection methods.

2.2.3. *Regressing the model equation for forecast and performing interpolation tests (Step 3)*

Next, I used the principal components estimated in Section 2.2.2 as explanatory variables of actual values of GRP, using the ordinary least squares method. I used real GRP values ranging from fiscal 1996 to 2011 as the explained variables (although, for the reason stated above, Shiga Prefecture's range was from 1998 to 2011). On the other hand, we examined all possible combinations of *n* principal components for the explanatory variable set and selected the best combination for my forecast model based on AIC tests.

Table 1. Selected monthly statistics

	Osaka	Hyogo	Kyoto	Shiga	Nara	Wakayama
Number of statistics	7	9	6	7	7	9
Employment						
Effective ratio of job offers to applicants	☼	☼	☼	☼	☼	☼ (※[1])
					☼ (※[2])	☼ (※[3])
Index of non-scheduled working hours	☼	☼				☼ (※[4])
Share of non-scheduled cash earnings						☼
Number of employment insurance recipients			☼			
Consumption						
Sales of large retail stores (per sales floor area)	☼ (※[4] • ※[5])	☼ (※[5])	☼ (※[4])	☼ (※[4])	☼	☼ (※[4])
Imports on customs basis	☼					
Production						
Index of industrial production	☼	☼	☼	☼	☼	☼
		☼ (※[6])				
Index of shipments of producers' goods	☼					
Index of operating ratio					☼	

Earnings ratio of firms		☼				
Index of inventory rate				☼		
Investment						
Floor area of ground-breaking construction		☼	☼	☼	☼ (※[7])	☼ (※[8])
Other						
Electricity consumption of major customers (Kansai area)	☼	☼		☼		☼
Nikkei Commodity Price Index (42 items) (whole nation)			☼	☼	☼	☼

Notes:
[1] The effective number of job offers.
[2] The effective ratio of the number of jobs which are successfully filled by job seekers to job offers.
[3] Osaka's effective ratio of job offers to applicants.
[4] The ratio to the same month of the previous year.
[5] Only for department stores.
[6] Index of machine industry production.
[7] Only for 11 industries.
[8] Only for new housing.

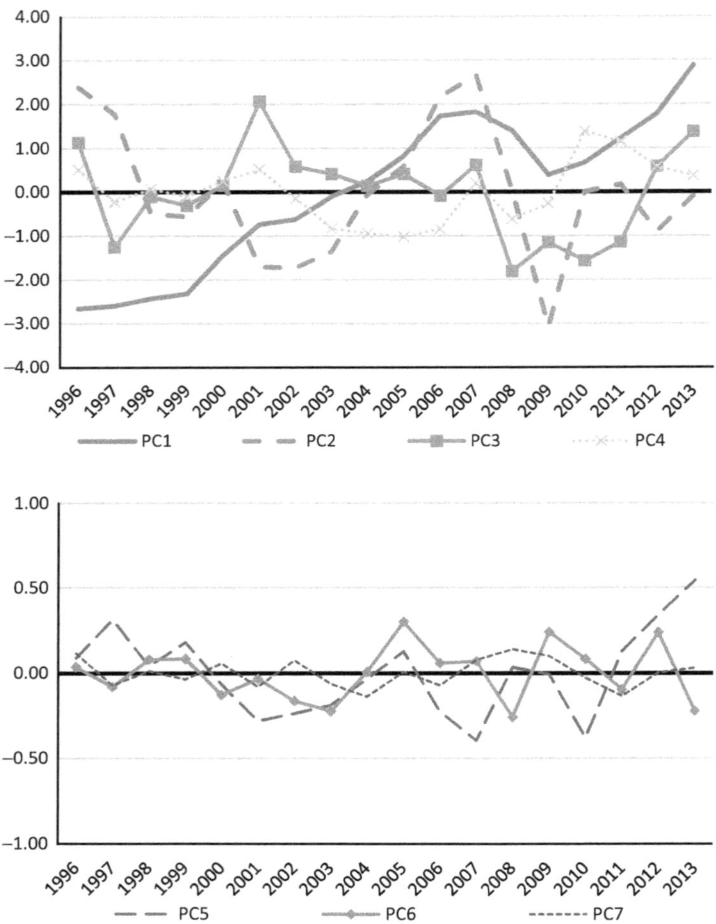

Figure 2. Principal components of economic fluctuations in Osaka prefecture

The results of my AIC tests are shown in Table 2. I found that the principal components that had the best results were not necessarily those with a relatively high contribution level (PC1–4). In fact, for every Kansai prefecture except for Kyoto, PCs 5 and above were chosen. For example, for Osaka Prefecture, PC1 was rejected, while PC5–7 were chosen.

The adjusted coefficients of determination (the adjusted R-squared values) of Hyogo, Kyoto, and Shiga were more than 0.9, whereas Osaka and Nara's were 0.81–0.82, and Wakayama's was 0.78. I will consider

Table 2. The regression models selected by AIC

Variable	Coefficient	Std. error	*t*-Statistic	Prob.
Osaka				
cons	38749521.89	91104.15	425.33	0.00
PC 2	418376.63	55361.66	7.56	0.00
PC 3	188139.14	89808.90	2.09	0.06
PC 5	717255.52	453345.50	1.58	0.14
PC 6	−832059.16	577735.03	−1.44	0.18
PC 7	2077683.21	994732.63	2.09	0.06
Adjusted R-squared		0.81		
Akaike info criterion		28.60		
Durbin–Watson stat.		2.34		
Hyogo				
cons	19422688.77	37727.47	514.82	0.00
PC 1	123840.55	15996.27	7.74	0.00
PC 2	261347.04	23720.16	11.02	0.00
PC 3	−81608.25	42698.43	−1.91	0.09
PC 4	107463.81	68097.84	1.58	0.15
PC 6	309026.82	105302.44	2.93	0.02
PC 8	263752.86	210164.66	1.25	0.24
Adjusted R-squared		0.94		
Akaike info criterion		26.84		
Durbin–Watson stat.		3.44		
Kyoto				
cons	9801754.60	32585.96	300.80	0.00
PC 1	270421.05	18915.24	14.30	0.00
PC 2	−650014.47	25836.81	−2.52	0.03
Adjusted R-squared		0.93		
Akaike info criterion		26.53		
Durbin–Watson stat.		2.23		

(*Continued*)

Table 2. (*Continued*)

Variable	Coefficient	Std. error	t-Statistic	Prob.
Shiga				
cons	5949367.72	17233.14	345.23	0.00
PC 1	256465.88	9057.53	28.32	0.00
PC 2	−96533.88	13582.20	−7.11	0.00
PC 3	−37663.01	17774.44	−2.12	0.07
PC 4	−153619.18	22903.37	−6.71	0.00
PC 7	−195266.25	119028.75	−1.64	0.14
Adjusted R-squared		0.99		
Akaike info criterion		25.21		
Durbin–Watson stat.		1.56		
Nara				
cons	3769795.17	9360.34	402.74	0.00
PC 1	−14005.40	4555.39	−3.07	0.01
PC 2	47605.31	7147.48	6.66	0.00
PC 3	−78740.86	21318.35	−3.69	0.00
PC 5	67228.43	39989.82	1.68	0.12
PC 7	−520429.35	210952.67	−2.47	0.03
Adjusted R-squared		0.82		
Akaike info criterion		24.12		
Durbin–Watson stat.		2.26		
Wakayama				
cons	3583894.543	11156.9926	321.224069	0.00
PC 1	36432.37512	5808.77368	6.27195638	0.00
PC 3	38947.45692	10137.4174	3.84195061	0.00
PC 6	76245.69955	26751.9522	2.85009853	0.02
PC 7	−44572.69241	29081.3247	−1.5326913	0.15
Adjusted R-squared		0.78		
Akaike info criterion		24.42		
Durbin–Watson stat.		2.38		

Notes: The cons means a constant term. The PC means principal component.

Table 3. Results of interpolation tests

	Osaka	Hyogo	Kyoto	Shiga	Nara	Wakayama
MAPE of levels of real GRP (%)	0.60	0.45	0.87	0.62	0.62	0.81
MAPE of real growth rates (%)	0.94	0.90	1.37	0.79	1.08	1.30
(Reference) Adjusted R-squared	0.81	0.94	0.93	0.99	0.82	0.78

Note: MAPE means the mean absolute percentage error between actual values and predicted ones.

these results in conjunction with the results of interpolation tests, as shown in Table 3. The MAPE of levels of real GRP in each prefecture was less than 1%, and the average MAPE of real GRP for all prefectures was 0.66%, a reasonable result.

Next, we examined the MAPE of real GRP growth rates. Osaka, Hyogo and Shiga's real GRP growth rates had a MAPE of less than 1%, Nara's was about 1%, Wakayama's and Kyoto's was 1.3%, and the average of all prefectures was 1.06%. Wakayama's adjusted R-squared, stated above, was the worst among the six prefectures, but its MAPE was not.

My above results confirm that making a model that can forecast the levels and growth rates of real GRP with a high degree of accuracy is possible even when restricted by a small number of samples and limited available statistics.

2.2.4. *Quick estimation of GRP (Step 4)*

Using regressions of real GRP and principal component sets for the period from fiscal 1996 to 2011 (for Shiga, fiscal 1998 to 2011), we extrapolated the principal component values for fiscal 2012 and 2013, then by performing constant term adjustments, I was able to forecast uncalculated real GRPs of each Kansai prefecture for 2 years recently (fiscal 2012 and 2013). The results are shown in Table 4.

These results provide an insight into the movements of the Kansai macroeconomy in fiscal 2012–13.

Fiscal 2012–13 was a turbulent period for the Japanese economy as a whole. Factors such as the recovery from the Great East Japan Earthquake

Table 4. Results of quick estimations

	Osaka	Hyogo	Kyoto	Shiga	Nara	Wakayama
Level of real GRP (trillion yen)						
FY2011 (Actual value)	38.45	19.71	10.46	6.43	3.75	3.68
FY2012 (Predicted value)	38.49	19.19	10.50	6.41	3.81	3.69
FY2013 (Predicted value)	39.55	19.35	10.57	6.54	3.89	3.77
Real growth rate (%)						
FY2011 (Actual value)	1.51	0.77	2.57	−0.54	−0.19	2.94
FY2012 (Predicted value)	0.09	−2.63	0.38	−0.40	1.46	0.44
FY2013 (Predicted value)	2.78	0.82	0.73	2.13	2.06	2.20

(which occurred in March 2011), the electricity crisis brought on by the nuclear accident, and changes to Japan's economic policies ("Abenomics" and the consumption tax increase) caused Japan's real GDP growth rate to fluctuate dramatically. During this period, Japan's real GDP growth rate recovered on the whole (growing by 0.7% in fiscal 2012 and 2.3% in fiscal 2013). But how did the Kansai economy fare in the same period? My quick estimation study has shown that the answer to this question can be found long before the final estimates of Kansai prefectural GRPs are released officially.

In fiscal 2012, GRP growth in each prefecture in the Kansai area except Nara was less than Japan's GDP growth (0.7%). Hyogo and Shiga in particular recorded negative GRP growth in fiscal 2012. This implies that the two prefectures' large manufacturing industries were strongly affected by the confusion in the supply chain and the electricity crisis precipitated by the Great East Japan Earthquake. We forecast that each prefecture subsequently realized positive growth in fiscal 2013. This implies the Kansai economy also benefited from "Abenomics" and time-switched purchases by consumers ahead of the consumption tax increase in April 2014.

3. Test of Prediction Accuracy

The previous sections showed how to make quick estimations of the levels and growth rates of real GRP using a modified version of the high-frequency forecast (principal components) model and applied this method to make quick estimates of Kansai prefectures' GRPs. It was also confirmed through interpolation tests that this estimation model reproduces actual GRP well.

This section will further test the accuracy of this forecast method's predictions. This test is performed by forecasting the real GRP value for the last fiscal year when real GRP was announced officially and then comparing forecast results to official results. In my case, the most recent GRP levels announced officially were those for fiscal 2011, and so we have forecast GRPs for fiscal 2011 using data from fiscal 1996–2010.[6]

This test is performed using almost the same method as is described above in Section 2.2, except that the period of the regression models' estimates is shortened by 1 year. This means that the monthly datasets and principal components used are the same as those used in Section 2, but there is a possibility that the combination of principal components chosen by the AIC could differ.

Table 5 presents the results of my AIC test on regression models for fiscal 2011 GRP. It shows that Shiga and Wakayama prefecture's combination of principal components has changed from those found in Table 2. However, each prefecture's adjusted R-squared values have not changed significantly, indicating that the accuracy of the model has not changed dramatically.

Table 6 shows the results of interpolation tests on these regression models.

Compared to the MAPE in Table 3 that was presented in Section 2, the MAPE values for Osaka, Hyogo, Kyoto, and Nara have remained at relatively similar levels, and the MAPE for Wakayama has improved. Shiga prefecture's MAPE worsened, but only slightly, to 1.02%. This demonstrates that MAPEs for this forecast model is much the same as MAPEs for the forecast model used in Section 2.

Table 7 shows the results of the comparison between forecasted real GRP levels and actual real GRP levels for fiscal 2011. As the absolute percentage error (APE) values of Osaka, Hyogo, and Shiga are less than 0.5%, I can confirm that our forecasted 2011 GRP for these prefectures was very close to the actual GRP levels. Kyoto is about 1% and Nara is about 1.3%, which seems a positive result. However, the APE for my

[6] However, the data we used for Shiga prefecture were from fiscal 1998–2010.

Table 5. Results of AIC tests of the model for forecasting 2011 GRP

Variable	Coefficient	Std. error	t-Statistic	Prob.
Osaka				
cons	38754079.29	99823.80	388.22	0.00
PC 2	418609.58	58286.34	7.18	0.00
PC 3	184469.49	97130.77	1.90	0.09
PC 5	730335.28	483755.55	1.51	0.17
PC 6	−849604.15	617390.13	−1.38	0.20
PC 7	1999745.13	1149518.05	1.74	0.12
Adjusted R-squared		0.80		
Akaike info criterion		28.72		
Durbin–Watson stat.		2.32		
Hyogo				
cons	19425412.97	43813.52	443.37	0.00
PC 1	124943.36	18438.07	6.78	0.00
PC 2	259996.72	26655.33	9.75	0.00
PC 3	−85142.55	50879.48	−1.67	0.13
PC 4	108928.71	72769.60	1.50	0.17
PC 6	318253.78	127057.44	2.50	0.04
PC 8	276044.23	236900.82	1.17	0.28
Adjusted R-squared		0.94		
Akaike info criterion		26.96		
Durbin–Watson stat.		3.40		
Kyoto				
cons	9791769.66	34570.46	283.24	0.00
PC 1	264650.33	20058.46	13.19	0.00
PC 2	−58562.44	26945.98	−2.17	0.05
Adjusted R-squared		0.93		
Akaike info criterion		26.55		
Durbin–Watson stat.		2.28		

(*Continued*)

Table 5. (*Continued*)

Variable	Coefficient	Std. error	*t*-Statistic	Prob.
Shiga				
cons	5910815.62	25217.49	234.39	0.00
PC 1	235983.11	13458.68	17.53	0.00
PC 2	−74173.16	18305.62	−4.05	0.00
PC 3	−163730.37	26218.86	−6.24	0.00
PC 4	−206734.02	94602.36	−2.19	0.07
PC 7	−423165.64	165543.95	−2.56	0.04
Adjusted R-squared		0.98		
Akaike info criterion		25.27		
Durbin–Watson stat.		2.20		
Nara				
cons	3771659.98	10201.71	369.71	0.00
PC 1	−15150.39	5107.58	−2.97	0.02
PC 2	47453.95	7400.66	6.41	0.00
PC 3	−76671.00	22344.48	−3.43	0.01
PC 5	66913.42	41384.34	1.62	0.14
PC 7	−537574.96	220267.56	−2.44	0.04
Adjusted R-squared		0.82		
Akaike info criterion		24.20		
Durbin–Watson stat.		2.14		
Wakayama				
cons	3571724.587	12729.0156	280.597078	0.00
PC 1	31572.31743	6312.66804	5.0014221	0.00
PC 3	40932.59674	9855.24745	4.15338092	0.00
PC 5	29853.48671	23049.6399	1.23518235	0.23
PC 6	49259.08892	29847.0401	1.65038438	0.14
PC 7	−36276.35472	28429.8559	−1.275995	0.2378
PC 8	120196.9505	70500.6717	1.70490504	0.1266
Adjusted R-squared		0.79		
Akaike info criterion		24.40		
Durbin–Watson stat.		3.10		

Notes: The cons refer to a constant term. PC means principal component.

Table 6. Results of the interpolation tests on the model for forecasting 2011 GRP

	Osaka	Hyogo	Kyoto	Shiga	Nara	Wakayama
MAPE of levels of real GRP (%)	0.63	0.48	0.86	0.67	0.63	0.58
MAPE of real growth rates (%)	0.98	0.95	1.38	1.02	1.07	1.15
(Reference) Adjusted R-squared	0.80	0.94	0.93	0.99	0.82	0.78

Note: MAPE means the mean absolute percentage error between actual values and forecasted ones.

Table 7. Extrapolation test results

	Osaka	Hyogo	Kyogo	Shiga	Nara	Wakayama
APE of level of real GRP in 2011	0.31	0.16	1.11	0.00	1.36	1.94
APE of real growth rate in 2011	0.31	0.16	1.12	0.00	1.37	1.96

Note: APE means the absolute percentage error between actual value and forecasted one.

prediction of Wakayama's GRP was about 2%. Our model for Wakayama had good interpolation test scores, but its adjusted R-squared value are lower than those of other prefectures, indicating that we may have to improve the model used for it. In spite of this, overall, the average APE for our forecasts of Kansai prefectures' GRPs was 0.81% and average APE for real GRP growth rate forecasts was 0.82%, so we can confirm the high forecast accuracy of this method.

4. Conclusions

GRP is the most comprehensive statistic when it comes to understanding the conditions of a regional economy. However, official GRP statistics take time to be calculated and released. In Japan, prefectural GRP statistics are released almost 2 years after national GDP statistics. Some prefectures have tried to make quick estimates of their GRPs, but these attempts have not accurately predicted final GRP levels. This chapter has presented a new high-frequency forecast (principal component analysis) method that can be used to make accurate quick estimates of GRP levels. The important feature of this method is that it uses principal components to forecast GRP directly. I have shown in this chapter that this new forecast method can be used to select several underlying monthly statistics that are released immediately and reflect economic conditions well. The method is also useful because it uses AIC to select sets of explanatory variables in order to solve the problem of having a small sample size. My tests of the model's fit (interpolation tests) and its forecast accuracy (extrapolation tests) showed that the method can be used to accurately forecast the GRP of the six prefectures in the Kansai region of Japan.

I aim to continue to improve the accuracy of this method in future studies. In particular, I will attempt to reselect monthly data for my Wakayama GRP forecast model, which has room for improvement, and to increase the amount of usable past time series data available. However, although there is room for improvement in certain prefectures, this method has shown enough promise to suggest that economists should continue to apply the method in practical settings and advance its potential.

Currently, the Asia Pacific Institute of Research (APIR) calculates and releases quick estimates using this method every year. Moreover, Osaka prefecture has already applied this method to make estimates of its GRP. It used these estimates to devise growth strategies and evaluate its own policies. It may not be long before the method, which provides accurate forecasts of recent economic movements, spreads out to other prefectures and even further afield.

References

Inada, Y. (2010) "High Frequency Model vs. Consensus Forecast," in S. Ichimura and L. R. Klein (eds.), *Macroeconometric Modeling of Japan* (*Econometrics in the Information Age: Theory and Practice of Measurement — Vol. 4*), Singapore and UK: World Scientific Publishing Co, pp. 393–409.

Klein, L. R. and Park, J. Y. (1993) "Economic Forecasting at High-frequency Intervals," *Journal of Forecasting*, 12, pp. 301–319.

Klein, L. R. and Park, J. Y. (1995) "The University of Pennsylvania Model for High-Frequency Economic Forecasting," *Economic and Financial Modeling*, Autumn, pp. 95–146.

Klein, L. R. and Sojo, E. (1989) "Combinations of High-frequency Data in Model-based Forecasting at the Federal Reserve Board," in L. R. Klein and J. Marquez (eds.), *Economics in Theory and Practice: An Eclectic Approach*, Dordrecht: Kluwer, pp. 3–16.

Chapter 5

Nationwide Development of Preliminary Estimates of Local Government GRPs

Hajime Watabe*

Nikkei Inc., Japan

1. Introduction

In this chapter, we apply the new method of estimating local government GRPs, developed in Chapter 4 to all 47 prefectures in Japan.

In the analysis of the Kansai area in Chapter 4, estimation was based on the economic variables which compose the Business Index of each Kansai prefecture. As the composition of the Business Index is determined by each prefecture's statistical committee, each prefecture's index reflects the unique economic situation of each prefecture, and is updated fairly quickly. Therefore, it is natural to use those variables as the basis for

*I wish to thank Yoshihisa Inada (Konan University) and Ryoh Ogawa (Osaka City University) for their kind support. I also wish to thank the participants of the Macro Model Conference 2014 for their useful comments. The conference was cosponsored by the Japan Center for Economic Research (JCER) and the Asia Pacific Institute of Research (APIR). The views expressed here are my own and do not necessarily reflect those of my employer. Any errors or omissions are the sole responsibility of the author.

preliminary GRP estimates. However, some prefectures do not calculate a Business Index. Moreover, acquiring the data of composition variables to make preliminary GRP estimates for the prefectures that do maintain a Business Index is often difficult due to the data not being publically available.

Nikkei Inc., a media organization with newspaper publishing at its core and one of the largest economic and financial data vendors in Japan (and employer of the author of this chapter), compiles major economic statistics such as industrial production and retail sales data for each prefecture. Nikkei maintains a database that contains those statistics called "NEEDS-CIDIc".[1] As data series in the NEEDS-CIDIc do not necessarily match those that make up the Business Index of each prefecture, the database does not fully cover the unique economic situation of each prefecture. However, the database does bear comparison with the Business Indexes offered by each prefecture in terms of number of series offered and frequency of updates. Because of this, we were able to apply the estimate method introduced in Chapter 4 to the data in the Nikkei's database and produce accurate estimates of prefectural GRPs.

We estimate the GRP of all 47 prefectures in Japan based on major indices in the NEEDS-CIDIc. To improve the accuracy of our estimates, we explore the following methods. First, we try to improve our in-sample accuracy by increasing the number of explanatory variables to nearly as many as the size of our sample period. However, we observe a tradeoff between in-sample accuracy and out-of-sample accuracy, that is, when in-sample accuracy improves, out-of-sample accuracy deteriorates. Second, we extend the estimation period by connecting old standard data for dependent GRP variables to new variable data. This extension improves the accuracy of our estimates to a certain extent. Third, instead of simply selecting equations with the largest R-squared value, we introduce a penalty term into the equation selection process to penalize in-sample and out-of-sample forecast error. This modification

[1] NEEDS stands for the "Nikkei Economic Electronic Database System", a brand name for the database service provided by Nikkei. NEEDS-CIDIc is a tool for calculating the composite index and diffusion index (the CI&DI Calculator), and also contains monthly economic data of each prefecture.

makes sign change for the actual and forecast growth rate far less frequent. Finally, we apply panel data analysis, which largely improves forecast accuracy.

The rest of the chapter is organized as follows. Section 2 describes the data used, Section 3 explains our estimation methods, Section 4 shows the results of our preliminary estimates on a prefecture-by-prefecture basis, Section 5 shows the results of our panel analysis, and Section 6 presents our conclusions.

2. Data

We use the following 13 series from the NEEDS-CIDIc as the basis for our preliminary GRP estimates:

— Index of Industrial Production (Mining and Manufacturing)
— Total building construction starts (by floor space)
— Loans and bills discounted
— Active job openings-to-applicants ratio
— New job openings-to-applicants ratio
— Non-scheduled hours worked, all industries
— Large-scale retail store sales value
— Total new passenger-car registrations
— Consumer price index
— Housing starts (by floor space)
— Number of business failures (surveyed by Tokyo Shoko Research, Ltd.)
— Number of beneficiaries in receipt of unemployment benefits
— Non-scheduled hours worked, Manufacturing

Because GRP is on fiscal-year basis, we first calculate fiscal-year-averages of these monthly series.[2]

[2] Japanese fiscal year begins in April and ends in March. Due to the Great East Japan Earthquake, two series (Non-scheduled hours worked of all industries and manufacturing) of three prefectures have missing values in early 2011 (specifically, March–April 2011 data of Iwate and Fukushima, and March–May 2011 data of Miyagi are missing), so we took average of non-missing values for 2010–2011 fiscal-year data of these prefectures.

For Hokkaido and Okinawa, we use 14 series, adding the "Large Industrial Power Consumption" data series.[3] Since large industrial power consumption is closely linked to economic activity, it would have been preferable to use this data series in our calculations for each prefecture. However, Hokkaido and Okinawa are the only prefectures where the local government's jurisdiction matches each electric power company's electric power distribution area, so we only use this data series for those two prefectures.

In some of the prefecture-by-prefecture analyses in Section 4, we use 9 instead of 13 series (10 instead of 14 for Hokkaido and Okinawa). In those calculations, we dropped the last 4 series in the above list, which are "Housing starts (by floor space)", "Number of business failures", "Number of beneficiaries in receipt of unemployment benefits", and "Non-scheduled hours worked, Manufacturing".[4]

Published data on the real GRP (reference year = 2005) were available only from the 2001 fiscal year (FY). So, as was done in Chapter 4, we linked these data to old data (reference year = 2000) using the ratios of FY2001 data as a link factor. This gave us access to data from FY1996 in our calculations. In the analysis in Section 4.2 and thereafter, we linked even older data so that we were able to include data from FY1985 onwards in our estimation calculations.

3. Estimation Methods

In this chapter, we principally followed the estimation method used in Chapter 4, and tried to improve the forecast accuracy by modifying the method. Specifically, we extracted the principal components from monthly data using principal component analysis, and regressed real GRP

---

[3] Large Industrial Power Consumption is a data series that has been sourced from NEEDS-ENERGY, another database produced by Nikkei. However, this series was discontinued in March 2016, as The Federation of Electric Power Companies of Japan stopped publishing the data.

[4] While each of these 4 series represents construction investment, corporate finance, labor market, and non-scheduled hours worked, the areas they represent are covered by remaining nine series.

on these components. We determined which combination of explanatory variables to employ by selecting the combination that has the highest explanatory power of all possible combinations. However, instead of the Akaike information criterion (AIC) used in Chapter 4, we used adjusted R-squared values to evaluate the explanatory power of our regressions.[5] This is because when we introduced a forecast-error penalty term into the evaluation of explanatory power in Section 4.3, we found that an adjusted R-squared value, which (generally) lies between 0 and 1, made it easier to formulate the evaluation function with the penalty term. Moreover, the AIC cannot be used to calculate in the panel analysis in Section 5 when a random effect model is added.

In the prefecture-by-prefecture estimations in Section 4, we only use principal components as explanatory variables in the regression calculations, as in Chapter 4. In the panel analysis in Section 5, we not only use principal components but also the year-on-year difference of those principal components, as well as the fiscal-year averages of original monthly data series and the year-on-year growth rates of the fiscal-year averages of original series. Throughout the various sets of variables we use in our panel analysis, we consistently use adjusted R-squared value as criteria to select the explanatory variables.

We evaluated forecast accuracy using out-of-sample forecasts of the FY2011 growth rate. Specifically, in our estimation equations we used GRP time series published in 2013, which contains data for up to FY2010, and forecast FY2011 GRP using those equations. We also used FY2011 data published in 2014 to verify the out-of-sample forecast accuracy of the data used in estimations. It should be noted that each time prefectural GRP is published, the past data are modified retrospectively. This means that the GRP data series used in our estimation equations is different from the data series to be forecasted. This, of course, has a negative effect on our out-of-sample forecasts. But, as our aim is to perform a preliminary estimation of the GRP, we have to estimate the next fiscal year's official GRP data from the data available at the time of estimation. This justified

[5]Explanatory variable combinations selected based on adjusted R-squared values can differ from combinations selected by the AIC in certain prefectures. Generally, these combinations differ for estimates of the GRP of only 4 or 5 out of the total 47 prefectures.

the use of unmodified GRP data published in 2013 to forecast the retrospectively modified versions of the GRP data published in 2014.

As was done in Chapter 4, we mainly used mean absolute percent error (MAPE) as a measure of forecast accuracy. We also used the number of prefectures whose growth rate had a wrong sign (that is, forecasted FY2011 growth rate was positive while actual FY2011 growth rate was negative, or vice versa), and a 47-prefecture cross-section correlation coefficient between the forecast and actual FY2011 growth rate, as measures of forecast accuracy.

4. Results of Prefecture-by-Prefecture Estimations

4.1. Tradeoff between in-sample and out-of-sample forecast accuracies

The merit of using principal component analysis is that the in-sample forecast error decreases as the number of explanatory variables increases. This is because principal components are orthogonal to each other. In an extreme case, if you increase the number of explanatory variables until their number is equal to the sample size, you can completely express the dependent variable as a linear combination of explanatory variables, so in-sample error becomes zero. However, in-sample minimization does not guarantee out-of-sample accuracy. In this section, we examined the relationship between in-sample accuracy and out-of-sample accuracy, and found that there is a tradeoff between the two.

The tradeoff can be seen in Figure 1, which shows two estimates of the Tokyo metropolitan prefecture GRP made with different numbers of explanatory variables. The sample period is 1996–2010, so the sample size is 15. In Figure 1(a), we used the 13 variables described in Section 2, and the number of principal components actually employed was also 13. The regression included a constant term, so the number of explanatory variables was very close to the sample size, i.e. the degree of freedom was 1. As a result, the in-sample MAPE became as low as 0.11% on a level basis, and 0.21% on a growth basis. However, as the figure shows, the behavior of the out-of-sample forecast was irregular. In FY2011, the first year of the out-of-sample forecast, GRP fell by nearly 20% from the

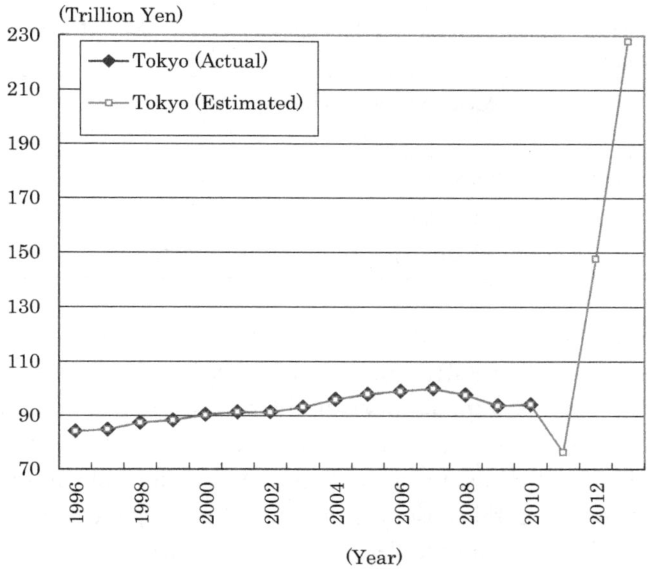

(a)

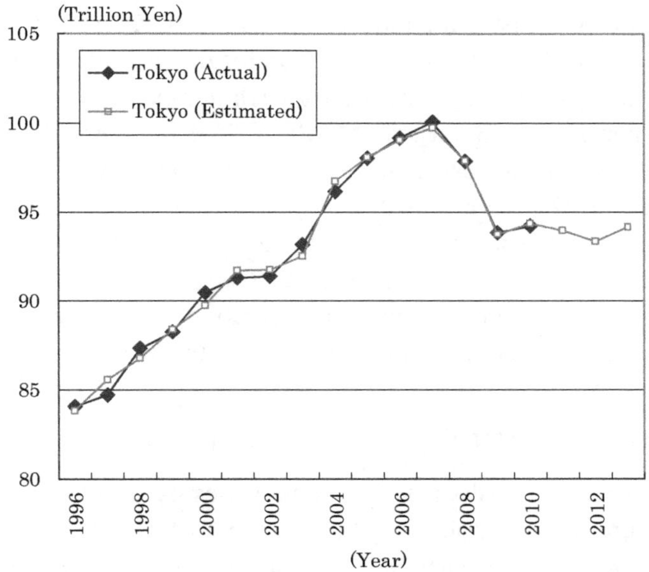

(b)

Figure 1. Tokyo metropolitan prefecture GRP estimate (a) 13 variables, (b) 9 variables.

Table 1. In-sample and out-of-sample MAPE of GRP forecasts for 47 prefectures

	Mean Absolute Percent Error (MAPE)	13 variables	9 variables
In-sample	Level error	0.28%	0.74%
	Growth error	0.50%	1.22%
Out-of-sample	FY2011 Growth Error	5.60%	2.46%

previous year. In FY2012, the second year, GRP almost doubled, and in the third year, FY2013, GRP grew by more than 50%. On the other hand, when the number of explanatory variables was reduced to nine, out-of-sample behavior became reasonable, as shown in Figure 1(b), although the in-sample MAPE became as high as 0.39% on a level basis and 0.73% on a growth basis. In this case, the number of principal components actually employed was 7, and the degree of freedom was 7.

It was observed that this pattern of extraordinary behavior from the out-of-sample forecast with reduced in-sample forecast error was not limited to Tokyo. Table 1 shows the 47-prefecture average MAPE for the in-sample and out-of-sample period for each number of variables. In the in-sample period, the 13-variable MAPE (0.28% on a level basis, 0.50% on a growth basis) was less than half of the 9-variable MAPE (0.74% on a level basis, 1.22% on a growth basis). However, for the out-of-sample FY2011 growth forecast, the 13-variable MAPE (5.60%) was more than twice the size of the 9-variable MAPE (2.46%).

Taking this phenomenon into consideration, we chose to use nine variables in the prefecture-by-prefecture estimates that follow.

4.2. The effects of extending the estimation period

As noted in Section 2, the real GRP data series used in the calculations presented up to this point begins from FY1996. This dataset was constructed by linking together 2005 reference-year data and 2000 reference-year data. Linking older 1995 base-year data and 1990 base-year data enables access to data as far back as FY1985. However, we used chain-weighted real GRP data in the previous calculations, and this kind of real

GRP data has not been calculated for 1990- and 1995-base-year data. Instead, only fixed-base-year real GRP data are available for this period. So, if we were to further link these data, it would be linking data that not only have a different base year but also were created using a different calculation method.[6] The question was, would the merit of using a longer time series outweigh the perverse effect that may arise from linking data found using different calculation methods?

The answer to that question was yes. When we estimated using real GRP data going back to FY1985, the forecast accuracy of the FY2011 growth rate improved. Specifically, the average MAPE for estimations of GRPs of the 47 prefectures became 2.08% for the estimate period of 1985–2010, compared with 2.46% for the estimate period of 1996–2010 reported in Table 1 in the previous section.

4.3. Introducing a penalty term into the evaluation function

Next, we attempted to further improve the accuracy of our forecasts by enhancing an evaluation function, which we maximized when selecting our regression equation, to account for the out-of-sample forecast error. Instead of simply using the adjusted R-squared value as the evaluation function, the following evaluation function L was used, to take the forecast error into account:

$$L = [\text{adjusted R-squared value}] - \lambda \times [\text{forecast error penalty term}].$$

The estimation period was also shortened by 2 years, from 1985–2010 to 1985–2008, and we incorporated the out-of-sample forecast error of 2009–2010 into the second term of the evaluation function, the penalty term. We also incorporated the in-sample forecast error into the second term. We set the penalty term as the weighted average of the 1985–1995 in-sample forecast error, the 1996–2008 in-sample forecast error, and the 2009–2010 out-of-sample forecast error, giving these samples weights of

[6] Although the fixed-based-year real GRP has been published along with the chain-weighted real GRP in recent series, our purpose is to forecast the chain-weighted real GRP, which has become the prevalent style of data.

0.5:1:6 in that order. We set the value of λ at 0.5, where λ is the coefficient of the penalty term.[7] As a result, the FY2011 growth rate forecast improved in terms of the number of prefectural growth rate forecasts with a wrong sign, which nearly halved from 17 to 9. However, the MAPE did not improve, worsening from 2.08% in the previous section to 2.30%. The main factor in this deterioration was Miyagi prefecture. The growth rate forecast for Miyagi became 20.54% in this calculation method (even though its actual growth rate was −1.06%). When Miyagi prefecture was excluded from estimates and an average of the remaining 46 prefectures was taken, the MAPE for the method presented in this section became 1.88%, which was a very slight improvement from the MAPE of the previous section's method, 1.94%.

5. Panel Analysis

5.1. The merits of panel analysis

At this point, we had estimated the GRP of each prefecture individually, and tried to improve the accuracy of the forecasts by fine-tuning the estimation method. As long as we estimated GRP on a prefecture-by-prefecture basis using the data presented in Section 2, further improvement of forecast accuracy was unlikely. Therefore, to further improve forecast accuracy, we had to either replace the estimation data, or adopt an alternative estimation method.

To make improvements by replacing data, we could have collected and selected data which reflected the unique situation of each prefecture. However, as noted in the introduction, making such a collection would have been very labor- and time-intensive, even for a few prefectures. Repeating that work for all the 47 prefectures would have been a prohibitively difficult task.

Of the alternative estimation methods, panel analysis was the most promising candidate. The aforementioned weak points of prefecture-by-prefecture analysis (the comparatively large cross-section number 47, and

[7]The weight of the forecast error in the penalty term and the value of λ were determined heuristically, so they are subject to further consideration and improvement.

the fact that we were using the same common economic variables across that cross-section due to limitations in the data) turned into strong points in panel analysis. Moreover, panel data is rather robust to multicollinearity problems. In prefecture-by-prefecture analysis, we conducted principal component analysis and used principal components as explanatory variables to avoid multicollinearity problems. In panel analysis, multicollinearity is unlikely to occur even if original series data are used as explanatory variables, because the method requires pooling and regressing data from different prefectures and years.

5.2. Results

Table 2 shows the result of our panel analysis. In these calculations, we used the 13 series presented in Section 2 for all prefectures including Hokkaido and Okinawa. Four different patterns of explanatory variables were tried: principal components, year-on-year difference of principal components, original series, and year-on-year growth rate of original series.[8] When we used the year-on-year difference of principal components or the growth rate of original series as our explanatory variables, we used the growth rate of real GRP as a response variable. For each combination of explanatory and response variables, we conducted five patterns of regression: simple pooled regression, pooled regression with cross-sectional fixed effects, pooled regression with cross-sectional random effects, pooled regression with time fixed effects, and pooled regression with time random effects.

As Table 2 demonstrates, when we used principal components as explanatory variables in pooled regression, our R-squared values became very low. Additionally, the correlation between forecast and actual growth for FY2011 was negative. Although the correlation between forecast and actual growth was also negative in Section 4.3 forecast, the absolute value of the negative correlation was larger in this pooled regression. The MAPE and the number of wrong signs also worsened when we used this method compared to when we used the method in Section 4.3. Although

[8] For "active job openings-to-applicants ratio" and "new job openings-to-applicants ratio" statistics, we used the year-on-year difference instead of year-on-year growth rate.

Table 2. Panel estimate results

Explanatory variables	Method	R-squared	FY2011 Growth forecast		
			MAPE (%)	Correlation coefficient	# of wrong signs
Principal components	Prefecture-by-prefecture estimate (Results of Section 4.3)	0.951	2.30	–0.180	9
Principal components	Simple pooled	0.004	2.59	–0.251	23
	Cross-sectional fixed effects	0.982	3.80	0.022	31
	Cross-sectional random effects	0.167	3.80	0.022	31
	Time fixed effects	–0.013	16.01	–0.171	42
	Time random effects	0.004	2.59	–0.251	23
Original series	Simple pooled	0.970	5.16	0.074	18
	Cross-sectional fixed effects	0.991	3.03	0.287	6
	Cross-sectional random effects	0.921	4.61	0.203	20
	Time fixed effects	0.977	44.93	0.135	42
	Time random effects	0.972	20.69	0.131	42
Year-to-year difference of principal components	Simple pooled	0.437	1.38	0.104	5

	Cross-sectional fixed effects	0.442	1.47	–0.123	5
	Cross-sectional random effects	0.440	1.40	0.048	5
	Time fixed effects	0.614	1.36	0.219	5
	Time random effects	0.114	1.33	0.380	5
Year-to-year growth rate of original series	Simple pooled	0.553	1.24	0.554	5
	Cross-sectional fixed effects	0.561	1.39	0.327	5
	Cross-sectional random effects	0.553	1.24	0.554	5
	Time fixed effects	0.642	1.27	0.546	5
	Time random effects	0.211	1.20	0.573	3

Notes: The R-squared values have been adjusted for degrees of freedom. For the prefecture-by-prefecture estimates (the results of Section 4.3), the R-squared value is the average of the regression equations for each of the 47 prefectures.

there were large differences in each prefecture's real GRP, we standardized all our explanatory variables as principal components in this analysis, which may have caused the fit of the regression equation to worsen.

When we introduced cross-sectional fixed effects, the R-squared increased substantially, and the correlation between the forecast and the actual growth rate became slightly positive. However, the MAPE and the number of wrong signs increased after cross-sectional fixed effects were introduced. While cross-sectional fixed effects explained the difference between the prefectural GRPs and increased the R-squared value, they did not lead to improvements in forecast accuracy. The results of cross-sectional random effects were very similar to those of cross-sectional fixed effects, except that the R-squared value was lower. Time fixed and random effects were not helpful either, and the results of the time random effects regression were identical to those found using simple pooled regression.

When the original time series data were used in place of principal components as explanatory variables, the R-squared value increased and approached unity, even for simple pooled regression. Seemingly, the differences in response variables were being explained without the help of cross-sectional effects because the value of explanatory variables such as "large-scale retail store sales value" was somewhat proportional to the value of real GRPs. But the MAPE of the original time series simple pooled regression method exceeded 5%, even worse than the MAPE of principal-component simple pooled regression (2.59%). The improvement of the MAPE was limited when cross-sectional effects were introduced, and the MAPE substantially worsened when we introduced time effects.

When we used year-on-year differences of principal components as an explanatory variable and the growth rate of real GRP as the response variable, the MAPE fell to less than 1.5%, although the R-squared value also decreased. The number of wrong signs remained at 5 out of 47 prefectures regardless of the regression method used. When we introduced time random effects, the R-squared value decreased to as low as 0.114, but the MAPE fell to its lowest level out of the five regression patterns and the correlation between forecast and actual growth increased to its highest level.

When we used the growth rate of the original series as an explanatory variable, we saw further improvements. With time random effects, the

Table 3. Regression equation with the best forecast accuracy

Sample Period: 1986–2010
Periods included: 25
Cross-sections included: 47
Total panel (balanced) observations: 1175

Variable	Coefficient	*t*-Statistic
C	1.3947	8.54
Index of industrial production	0.0887	6.86
Large-scale retail store sales value	0.0325	2.52
Consumer price index	0.0772	0.81
Loans and bills discounted	0.0496	4.47
Non-scheduled hours worked, manufacturing	0.0166	2.42
New job openings-to-applicants ratio	2.3023	5.99
The number of business failures	0.0112	4.31
Beneficiaries in receipt of unemployment benefits	–0.0254	–3.26
Housing starts, floor space	0.0258	3.64

R-squared	0.217
Adjusted R-squared	0.211
S.E. of regression	1.74
F-statistic	35.93
Durbin–Watson stat	2.03

Note: The response variable is the year-on-year growth rate of GRP. We used the year-on-year growth rate of each time series as explanatory variables, with the exception of "new job openings-to-applicants ratio", for which we used the year-on-year difference.

MAPE was 1.20%, and the correlation coefficient between forecast and actual growth was 0.573. This is the lowest MAPE and the highest correlation statistic among the analyses in this chapter. Even the number of wrong signs fell to 3 when we used this pattern. Table 3 shows the regression equation of this estimation method. For this equation, we selected 9 out of 13 candidate variables as explanatory variables. All the signs of the regression coefficients were consistent with economic intuition, except that of "the number of business failures", which was positive. All *t*-values exceeded 2 in absolute value, except that of the "Consumer Price Index."

5.3. Discussion

In sum, we obtained better results when the panel analysis was based on a growth rate rather than the value of an economic variable. Surprisingly, we even obtained good results from panel analysis using the year-on-year differences of principal components as explanatory variables. This means that there was a stable relationship between the principal components, which were extracted from the same set of monthly time series, and the real GRP across different prefectures. It should be noted, however, that using the growth rate of the original time series led to even better results. Principal component analysis was implemented in Chapter 4 mainly to account for the multicollinearity problem, but the panel analysis in this chapter presents another method of circumventing multicollinearity. If all the prefectures are estimated at once using panel analysis, fairly high estimation accuracy can be obtained, even with the original time series.

It should also be noted that the R-squared value does not indicate the accuracy of forecasts made using panel analysis, as can be seen in Table 2. For example, introducing time random effects into growth rate analysis leads to a decrease in the R-squared value, but forecast accuracy improves.[9]

The graphs in Figure 2 are scatter graphs showing our forecast growth rates and the actual growth rates of prefectural GRPs for FY2011. The data in Figure 2(a) were forecast using the prefecture-by-prefecture estimation method described in Section 4.3 (which excluded Miyagi). The data in Figure 2(b) were forecast using the panel analysis pattern that incorporates the growth rate of the original series and time random effects, which was the pattern with the highest forecast accuracy of this chapter's analyses. Forecast data are widely scattered in Figure 2(a), and concentrated in the 1–3% range in 2(b). Difference in forecast accuracy is demonstrated by the regression line, which is almost flat in 2(a), while sloping upward in 2(b).

To check the robustness of the superiority of the panel estimate over the prefecture-by-prefecture estimate, we repeated the forecasting procedure we conducted for FY2011 from FY2012 to FY2014, and averaged

[9] In addition to one-way fixed/random effects, we also tried two-way fixed/random effects, but the forecasts made using the regression equation with one-way time random effects remained most accurate. However, when the Hausman test was conducted, time random effects were rejected.

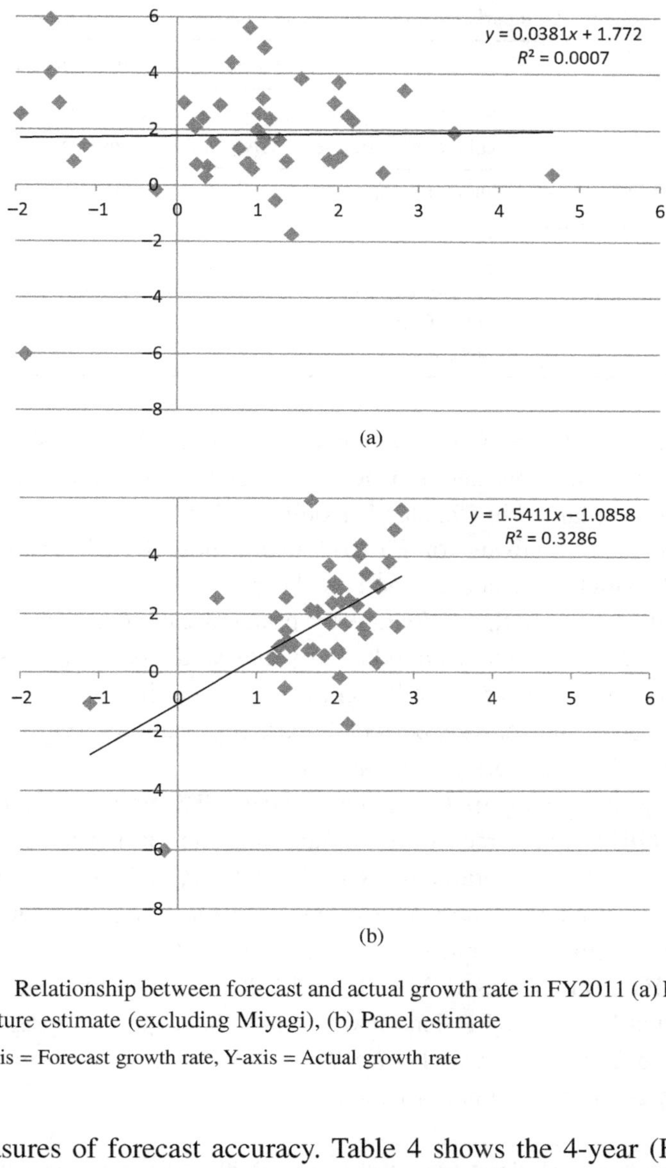

Figure 2. Relationship between forecast and actual growth rate in FY2011 (a) Prefecture-by-prefecture estimate (excluding Miyagi), (b) Panel estimate

Note: X-axis = Forecast growth rate, Y-axis = Actual growth rate

the measures of forecast accuracy. Table 4 shows the 4-year (FY2011–2014) averages of MAPE, correlation coefficient, and the number of wrong signs of each method. All three measures show that the panel estimate is still more accurate than the prefecture-by-prefecture estimate when averaged over 4 years.

Table 4. Comparison of two methods (FY2011–FY2014 average)

		FY2011–14 Growth forecast (Average)		
Method	Explanatory variables	MAPE (%)	Correlation coefficient	# of wrong signs
Prefecture-by-prefecture estimate (Section 4.3 method)	Principal components	2.55	0.160	14.5
Panel estimate with time random effects	Year-to-year growth rate of original series	1.73	0.393	13.25

Panel estimate method also enables us to use relatively short-period data. For example, four series of RDEI (Regional Domestic Expenditure Index) data explained in Chapter 1 is only available since 2002. When we conducted panel analysis for FY2011 using those RDEI series, MAPE was 1.50, which was not as good as the panel estimate of Section 5.2 (1.20), but better than the prefecture-by-prefecture estimate of Section 4.3 (2.30). Moreover, when we conducted panel analysis using those series for FY2012 and onwards, results seemed to be getting better along with the extension of the analysis period. Apparently, incorporating RDEI data is one line of future work to be pursued.

Finally, let us compare the sum of our best GRP estimates and the sum of actual GRPs. The forecast growth rate presented in Figure 2(b) can be used to estimate each prefecture's FY2011 GRP, and these forecasts in turn can be used to obtain an estimate for the national GDP growth in FY2011. Using this method, we estimated that the GDP growth rate in Japan in FY2011 increased 2.0% from FY2010. Adding up each prefecture's actual FY2011 GRP data, it was found that Japan's aggregate GRP growth rate for FY2011 was 1.9%.[10] This result suggests that our estimate was fairly accurate on a nationwide basis.[11]

[10]This growth rate is calculated using the data as of FY2011 GRPs publication (that is, the data used in the evaluation of Sections 4 and 5 results). When calculated using the data as of FY2014 GRPs publication (which is the most recent data at the time of this analysis), aggregate GRP growth rate for FY2011 was 2.0%.

[11]It should be noted that Japan's real GDP growth rate in FY2011 according to Cabinet Office data as of June 2014 (when FY2011 GRPs were published) was 0.3%, which differs

6. Conclusions

In this chapter, we applied the new method of estimating local government GRPs, developed in Chapter 4, to all 47 prefectures in Japan. When we tried to estimate each prefecture's GRP individually, it was observed that when in-sample accuracy was improved by increasing the number of explanatory variables, out-of-sample accuracy decreased. When we extended the estimation period by connecting the old-standard GRP data to current GRP data, forecast accuracy improved. Also, when we introduced a penalty term which penalized in-sample and out-of-sample forecast errors into the equation selection process, the number of prefectures for which forecast growth rate sign differed from actual growth rate sign almost halved.

When panel data analysis was used for estimation, forecast accuracy improved substantially compared to when prefectural GRP data was estimated individually. In particular, panel data estimates made using growth rate data lead to results with higher forecast accuracy than estimates made using value data of principal components or the original series. We argue that including panel data analysis into high-frequency forecasts makes it possible to forecast regional GRPs with relatively high accuracy and low cost, even when the number and variety of annual data available is limited. This approach should be regarded as a practical alternative to the approach used in Chapter 4, which requires a labor-intensive search of a set of statistics unique to each prefecture. However, there may be further room to improve the forecast accuracy of the approach presented here by either switching between panel analysis results and individual analysis results depending on the method that is most accurate for each prefecture, or combining the results of both methods in a proper way. We aim to investigate these methods in our future work.

---

from the growth rate we obtained by adding up GRP data by 1.6 percentage points. Although there is always difference between aggregate prefectural and national data, the average absolute difference between these two data sets from FY1995 to FY2010 is 0.8 percentage points. In FY2011, the fiscal year that began less than a month after the Great East Japan Earthquake, this gap widened to twice the average. One reason why aggregate prefectural data and national data differ is that additivity does not hold for chain-weighted real GRP, but apparently the earthquake exacerbated the gap in FY2011.

References

Inada, Y. (2009) "A High-Frequency Forecasting Model and Its Application to the Japanese Economy," in L. R. Klein (ed.), *The Making of National Economic Forecasts,* Edward Elgar, pp. 172–197.

Inada, Y. (2010) "High Frequency Model vs Consensus Forecast," S. Ichimura and L. R. Klein (eds.), *Macroeconometric Modeling of Japan* (*Econometrics in the Information Age: Theory and Practice of Measurement — Vol. 4*), Singapore and UK: World Scientific Publishing Co, pp. 393–409.

Index

T

U

CPSIA information can be obtained
at www.ICGtesting.com
Printed in the USA
LVHW06*2337100518
576813LV00003B/10/P

9 789813 232365